Majestic Heights, Kilimanjaro_s Secrets

Majestic Heights, Kilimanjaro_s Secrets

Solomon Raj

Noble Publishing

CONTENTS

INDEX 1

1. Chapter 1 3
2. Chapter 2 20
3. Chapter 3 40
4. Chapter 4 65
5. Chapter 5 89
6. Chapter 6 115
7. Chapter 7 137
8. Chapter 8 159
9. Chapter 9 182

INDEX

Chapter 1: Introduction to Majestic Heights

1.1 Introduce the breathtaking beauty of Majestic Heights, a fictional region at the base of Mount Kilimanjaro.

1.2 Set the scene with vivid descriptions of the landscape, wildlife, and the towering presence of Kilimanjaro.

1.3 Introduce the main characters and their connection to Majestic Heights.

Chapter 2: The Enigmatic Mountain

2.1 Explore the history and mystique surrounding Mount Kilimanjaro.

2.2 Delve into the local legends and myths that have been passed down through generations.

2.3 Introduce the concept of Kilimanjaro's secrets and the intrigue surrounding the mountain.

Chapter 3: The Protagonist's Arrival

3.1 The protagonist arrives in Majestic Heights, drawn by a mysterious calling or a personal quest.

3.2 Describe their initial impressions and interactions with the locals.

3.3 Establish the protagonist's goals and motivations for being in Majestic Heights.

Chapter 4: Unveiling the Hidden Treasures

4.1 The protagonist begins to uncover the secrets hidden within Majestic Heights.

4.2 Explore ancient artifacts, hidden caves, or mystical elements that hold clues to Kilimanjaro's secrets.

4.3 Introduce challenges and obstacles that the protagonist must overcome.

Chapter 5: Local Wisdom and Guidance

5.1 The protagonist seeks guidance from local elders, shamans, or knowledgeable figures.

5.2 Discover the wisdom passed down through generations about the mystical elements of Majestic Heights.

5.3 Develop relationships between the protagonist and the community.

Chapter 6: Facing Challenges

6.1 The protagonist encounters challenges and trials on their quest.

6.2 Develop tension and suspense as they navigate through difficult terrain or face adversaries.

6.3 Highlight the resilience and determination of the protagonist.

Chapter 7: Revelation at the Summit

7.1 The climax of the story occurs as the protagonist reaches the summit of Kilimanjaro.

7.2 Unveil the long-guarded secrets and the true purpose of Majestic Heights.

7.3 Tie together the various elements of the story, providing a satisfying resolution to the mystery.

Chapter 8: Integration and Transformation

8.1 Explore the aftermath of the revelation and how it impacts the protagonist and the community.

8.2 Highlight personal growth, newfound wisdom, and the integration of the revealed secrets into the lives of the characters.

8.3 Resolve any lingering conflicts or unanswered questions.

Chapter 9: Reflection and Legacy

9.1 Conclude the story with reflections on the journey and the significance of the secrets uncovered.

9.2 Consider the legacy left behind by the protagonist and the impact on Majestic Heights.

9.3 End with a sense of closure and the promise of new beginnings for the characters and the region.

Chapter 1

Introduction to Majestic Heights

Magnificent Levels, a rambling territory settled in the midst of the undulating shapes of nature's material, fills in as a demonstration of human resourcefulness and design wonder. This private ideal world, situated on the edges of the clamoring city, remains as an encapsulation of extravagance, quietness, and vanguard plan. As one leaves on an excursion through the passageways of Superb Levels, the consistent mix of lavishness and normal excellence becomes clear, making a desert spring of serenity where current residing unites with the immortal charm of the encompassing scene.

The beginning of Lofty Levels can be followed back to a visionary consortium of designers, metropolitan organizers, and engineers who looked to rethink the worldview of contemporary living. Their aggregate desire was to make a shelter that rises above the ordinary limits of private design, raising the idea of home to an unmatched pinnacle. With fastidious tender loving care and a guarantee to orchestrating with the climate, Superb Levels arose as a symbol of complexity, where each component blends to make a residing experience that is both liberal and feasible.

SOLOMON RAJ

Settled against the scenery of moving slopes and verdant woodlands, Grand Levels was decisively situated to exploit the normal quality that encompasses it. The designers, aware of the significance of area, guaranteed that occupants would be welcomed by all encompassing vistas that change with the seasons. Whether it be the rich greens of spring, the searing shades of pre-winter, or the quiet cover of winter snow, Magnificent Levels is a material whereupon nature paints its steadily developing work of art.

The compositional plan of Glorious Levels is an ensemble of contemporary style and traditional sensibilities. The private pinnacles, each a transcending demonstration of present day designing, stand as one with the scene. Glass veneers flawlessly converge with the encompassing foliage, permitting occupants to delight in unhindered perspectives while encouraging a feeling of unity with the normal world. The modelers' accentuation on ease and open spaces has brought forth a climate where light and air dance easily, making an ethereal feeling that rises above the limits of traditional residing spaces.

As one explores the fastidiously finished grounds of Grand Levels, the obligation to natural maintainability becomes obvious. The rambling nurseries, enhanced with native vegetation, go about as a safe-haven for the two inhabitants and neighborhood fauna. Maintainability isn't only a trendy expression at Magnificent Levels; a directing way of thinking pervades each feature of its presence. From water gathering frameworks to energy-effective lighting, the territory remains as a paragon of capable metropolitan turn of events.

The core of Grand Levels lies in its mutual spaces, carefully created to cultivate a feeling of local area and gaiety. The focal square, a clamoring center of action, fills in as a gathering point where occupants can participate in friendly cooperations, widespread developments, and sporting pursuits. The court's plan, motivated by the greatness of noteworthy town squares, is a sign of approval for the revered practice of mutual living, rethought for the cutting edge period.

The private units inside Magnificent Levels are a concentrate in richness and ergonomic plan. The insides, washed in normal light, are a demonstration of the designers' unfaltering obligation to making spaces that flawlessly mix structure and capability. High roofs, far reaching windows, and best in class apparatuses describe the homes, guaranteeing that each habitation inside Glorious Levels is a casing of solace and style. The reconciliation of savvy home advancements further raises the residing experience, furnishing inhabitants with unrivaled command over their residing spaces.

Past the compositional wonders and rich conveniences, Lofty Levels is a stronghold of inclusivity and variety. The engineers intentionally looked to make a microcosm of society where occupants hail from fluctuated foundations, callings, and age gatherings. This purposeful variety has led to an energetic and dynamic local area, where the trading of thoughts, social subtleties, and shared encounters enhance the existences of those inside Superb Levels.

The obligation to comprehensive prosperity reaches out to the sporting offices inside Superb Levels. The wellness community, furnished with cutting edge gear, coaxes wellness fans to set out on an excursion of wellbeing and essentialness. For those leaned towards additional comfortable pursuits, the spa and health focus offers a reprieve from the afflictions of day to day existence. Great Levels isn't only a home; it is an all encompassing safe-haven where the whole self track down balance.

With regards to the ethos of contemporary metropolitan living, Magnificent Levels brags an organized choice retail outlets and feasting foundations. The business region inside the territory is a microcosm of cosmopolitan living, offering occupants the comfort of shopping, feasting, and diversion inside arm's scope. The engineers' premonition in coordinating business spaces inside the private territory mirrors a nuanced comprehension of the cutting edge occupant's craving for comfort without settling for less on the personal satisfaction.

The charm of Magnificent Levels reaches out past its actual limits; it is a way of life organized to take care of the insightful preferences of its inhabitants. The people group occasions schedule is a demonstration of this responsibility, including a different cluster of social, sporting, and instructive exercises. From workmanship displays and melodic exhibitions to studios and workshops, Lofty Levels tries to develop a climate where occupants can participate in an embroidery of encounters that enhance and jazz up their day to day routines.

The security and protection of occupants are central at Lofty Levels. A best in class security foundation, including observation frameworks, secure passages, and prepared work force, guarantees that occupants can partake in a serene living climate without settling on wellbeing. The territory's obligation to encouraging a solid climate isn't only bound to actual security; it reaches out to the profound prosperity of inhabitants, making a space where people and families can flourish.

Lofty Levels isn't simply a private territory; it is a demonstration of the persevering through soul of human desire and development. As one navigates its finished roads, takes in the all encompassing perspectives from the private pinnacles, and draws in with the energetic local area, it becomes obvious that Great Levels is more than the amount of its design miracles and conveniences. It is a no nonsense element that develops with the rhythmic movement of its inhabitants' lives, a material whereupon the tales of incalculable people interweave to make a story of aggregate victory and shared yearnings.

All in all, Lofty Levels remains as a reference point of contemporary residing, a safe-haven where extravagance, manageability, and local area meet. Its building magnificence, natural care, and obligation to all encompassing prosperity position it as a worldview for the fate of metropolitan living. Superb Levels isn't just a private territory; it is a demonstration of the human ability to dream, develop, and make spaces that rise above the standard, enticing inhabitants to set out on an excursion of unrivaled living.

1.1 Introduce the breathtaking beauty of Majestic Heights, a fictional region at the base of Mount Kilimanjaro.

Settled at the foundation of the grand Mount Kilimanjaro, Superb Levels divulges itself as a domain of unmatched regular wonder. This imaginary district, an amicable mix of stunning scenes and untamed wild, catches the embodiment of immaculate excellence. As the sun rises, giving occasion to feel qualms about its brilliant gleam the undulating fields and the famous outline of Kilimanjaro, Lofty Levels arises as a demonstration of the crude, untamed loftiness of nature.

The geological material of Grand Levels is a masterstroke of nature's imaginativeness. Lavish, moving slopes decorated with a dynamic embroidery of native greenery stretch as may be obvious. The air, fresh and strengthening, conveys with it the fragrance of wildflowers and the far off mumble of flowing water. The scene, an intricate interwoven pattern of greens and natural tones, welcomes investigation and thought, coaxing occupants and guests the same to submerge themselves in its stunning excellence.

At the core of Great Levels lies the confounding Mount Kilimanjaro, its transcending presence creating a big-hearted shaded area over the locale. The snow-covered highest point, unendingly shimmering in the daylight, remains as an image of immortality and perseverance. Great Levels owes quite a bit of its charm to this famous milestone, as Kilimanjaro's glory impacts each part of life in this imaginary district, molding its character and characterizing its musicality.

The widely varied vegetation of Magnificent Levels paint a distinctive scene of biodiversity. Native trees, their branches coming to towards the sky, give shade to the bunch of animals that call this locale home. The resonant orchestra of birdsong consumes the space, making a characteristic soundtrack that goes with inhabitants on their everyday excursions. The made up environment of Magnificent Levels is a fragile dance of life, where every species assumes a urgent part in keeping up with the natural equilibrium of this immaculate territory.

Winding waterways and completely clear streams wander through Grand Levels, their delicate mumbles winding around stories of old scenes and the endless entry of time. These water bodies, overflowing with life, act as a wellspring of food and motivation for those lucky enough to call Magnificent Levels home. The waterways, mirroring the sky blue skies and the verdant environmental factors, are symbolic of the district's obligation to safeguarding its regular legacy.

The private design of Superb Levels honors the scene, consistently incorporating with the regular environmental factors. Specked along the slopes, the homes are intended to give unhampered perspectives on the amazing display that unfurls past their walls. Huge, all encompassing windows welcome the outside in, obscuring the limits between the inside and outside spaces. The structural stylish is a marriage of current complexity and rural appeal, making a visual orchestra that resounds with the regular magnificence of Magnificent Levels.

The soul of Lofty Levels is embodied in its obligation to supportability and ecological stewardship. The draftsmen and organizers behind this made up heaven have embraced eco-accommodating works on, guaranteeing that the improvement proceeds with caution on the land it possesses. From energy-proficient structure plans to squander reusing drives, Glorious Levels remains as a guide of dependable turn of events, showing the way that human residence can coincide agreeably with nature.

Occupants of Superb Levels are not simply occupants; they are overseers of a no nonsense biological system. The people group is pervaded with a significant feeling of ecological cognizance, with drives going from tree-establishing efforts to untamed life protection projects. The occupants of Grand Levels comprehend that their prosperity is unpredictably associated with the strength of the climate, and this mindfulness penetrates each part of their day to day routines.

The people group of Glorious Levels is an embroidery woven with strings of variety and inclusivity. People from various different backgrounds, drawn by the charm of this made up heaven, meet up to make an agreeable mosaic of societies, customs, and points of view. The mutual spaces, decisively positioned to amplify communication, act as mixtures where occupants share stories, manufacture kinships, and commend the rich woven artwork of human experience.

Sporting spaces inside Lofty Levels are intended to supplement the regular excellence that encompasses them. Stops and assembling regions are decisively situated to offer stunning perspectives on Kilimanjaro and the broad fields underneath. Whether participating in collective exercises or looking for isolation amidst nature, occupants of Glorious Levels track down comfort and delight in the cautiously arranged sporting spaces that spot the scene.

The imaginary territory flaunts an instructive foundation that mirrors its obligation to comprehensive turn of events. Schools inside Great Levels are not only foundations of learning; they are centers of motivation, cultivating imagination, decisive reasoning, and a profound appreciation for the normal world. The educational program is intended to impart a feeling of ecological obligation, supporting an age of people who figure out the fragile harmony among progress and conservation.

Great Levels, as a flourishing center of culture and expressions, praises the inventive soul that lives inside its local area. The imaginary area has a variety of far-reaching developments, from craftsmanship presentations to live events, where occupants and guests the same can submerge themselves in the rich embroidered artwork of human articulation. Glorious Levels isn't simply an actual space; it is a material whereupon the social character of its occupants is painted and celebrated.

The business and exchange inside Superb Levels are driven by a guarantee to maintainability and moral practices. Nearby craftsmans and organizations, motivated by the regular magnificence that encompasses them, add to a lively commercial center where handcrafted creates, natural produce, and eco-accommodating items become the dominant focal point. The business regions of Superb Levels are not simply monetary center points; they are expansions of the district's ethos, exemplifying the standards of mindful utilization and local area support.

Glorious Levels, albeit an imaginary creation, reverberates with the general longing for an association with nature, a feeling of local area, and a promise to supportable living. As the sun sets over Kilimanjaro, projecting a warm, brilliant shade over the scene, Lofty Levels remains as a demonstration of the getting through excellence of immaculate wild and the limitless capability of amicable concurrence among humankind and the regular world. It is where the soul of experience meets the serenity of home, welcoming all who enter to turn out to be important for a story that praises the stunning magnificence of Magnificent Levels.

1.2 Set the scene with vivid descriptions of the landscape, wildlife, and the towering presence of Kilimanjaro.

In the core of East Africa, where the sun kisses the earth with its brilliant warmth, lies the stunning scene of Glorious Levels. This charming district, settled at the foundation of the notable Mount Kilimanjaro, divulges a universe of regular ponders that enamor the faculties and mix the spirit. As the primary light of sunrise washes the land in tones of pink and orange, Great Levels arises as a sanctuary of untamed magnificence, an orchestra of varieties and surfaces that dance as one with the rhythms of nature.

The landscape of Grand Levels is a work of art of variety, a material painted with moving slopes, verdant valleys, and open fields that stretch towards the skyline. Every undulation of the scene recounts an account of time's section, set apart by the delicate touch of the breeze and the patient chiseling of raindrops. The slopes, delegated with emerald-green grasses that influence in the breeze, make a hypnotizing interwoven that covers the earth in an embroidery of life.

Veins of perfectly clear waterways and streams wind through the land, their waters mirroring the sky blue sky and reflecting the rich foliage that lines their banks. The streams, with their delicate mumbles, describe stories of hundreds of years gone via, conveying with them the mysteries of Glorious Levels. They wander through the scene, giving food to the greenery that call this locale home, and offering a peaceful background to the energetic embroidery of life unfurling around them.

The greenery of Glorious Levels is a festival of nature's variety, with a variety of native trees and plants that add profundity and character to the scene. Transcending acacias, their branches extending towards the sky, cast dappled shadows on the ground underneath.

Baobab trees, old sentinels with goliath trunks, stand as quiet observers to the progression of time. Wildflowers of each and every variety, from fragile blues to red hot reds, lay out the scene with a range that changes with the seasons, making a consistently moving display of excellence.

As the day unfurls, Superb Levels wakes up with the ensemble of avian voices. Birds of heap tones and sizes consume the space with their musical calls, making a characteristic symphony that resounds through the slopes and valleys. Superb birds take off high over, their sharp eyes checking the scene for prey, while lively sunbirds dance among the blooms, their radiant plumage getting the daylight. Superb Levels is a shelter for birdwatchers, offering an unparalleled view to the theater of avian life that works out against the setting of Kilimanjaro.

The untamed life of Grand Levels wanders unreservedly, a demonstration of the district's obligation to saving its normal legacy. Agile giraffes, their necks going after the delicate leaves of acacia trees, get with an easy class across the fields. Transcending elephants, their tusks sparkling in the daylight, cross antiquated relocation courses went down through ages. Superb lions, their brilliant coats mixing consistently with the savannah grasses, study their domains with grand power. Lofty Levels is a safe-haven for the collective of animals, where the sensitive harmony between hunter and prey unfurls in a dance ancient.

At the core of this entrancing display stands the transcending goliath that is Mount Kilimanjaro. This magnificent top, with its snow-covered highest point puncturing the cerulean sky, creates a kindhearted shaded area over Lofty Levels. Kilimanjaro, a lethargic spring of gushing lava and the most elevated unsupported mountain on the planet, isn't just a topographical component; an otherworldly presence shapes the personality of the whole district. The ice sheets on Kilimanjaro flicker like gems, their flawless excellence an unmistakable difference to the warm shades of the encompassing scene.

The snows of Kilimanjaro, a remnant of a former period, have seen the progression of time in Superb Levels. They are a wellspring of life, taking care of the streams that move through the locale and supporting the rich biodiversity that flourishes in this normal heaven. The nearby networks, with profound veneration for the mountain, consider Kilimanjaro a land wonder as well as a hallowed substance that holds the way in to the thriving and prosperity of Great Levels.

The foundation of Kilimanjaro is decorated with a mosaic of environments, every one a microcosm of life adjusted to the elevation and environment. From the thick montane woods, where greenery covered trees make a charmed domain, to the snow capped glades, where strong plants grip to rough inclines, Kilimanjaro's lower comes to are an embroidery of biodiversity. Lofty Levels, in the shadow of this giant mountain, benefits from the biological variety that Kilimanjaro supports, making a scene that isn't just outwardly dazzling yet in addition naturally hearty.

The magnificence of Kilimanjaro stretches out past its actual loftiness; a signal draws globe-trotters, pilgrims, and searchers from around the world. Grand Levels, as the watchman at Kilimanjaro's base, invites the individuals who try to vanquish the highest point or the people who long to encounter the significant association among mankind and nature. Kilimanjaro, with its difficult pinnacles and remarkable vistas, is an image of perseverance, flexibility, and the dauntless soul of the people who hope against hope.

As the sun sets over Glorious Levels, projecting a warm shine on the scene, Kilimanjaro wears a shroud of delicate nightfall shades. The stars, unhindered by the city lights, sparkle in the immense African sky, making a divine scene that reflects the miracles of the earth underneath. The night in Great Levels isn't a period of dimness yet a material on which the groups of stars recount stories, and the hints of the nighttime animals consume the space with a bedtime song that serenades the locale into a peaceful sleep.

In each dawn and dusk, in the dance of the waterways and the murmurs of the breeze, Grand Levels uncovers itself as a living embroidery of nature's marvels. Kilimanjaro, remaining as a quiet sentinel, looks after this charmed domain, where the excellence of the scene, the variety of untamed life, and the otherworldly presence of the mountain join to make an encounter that rises above the standard. Glorious Levels is a demonstration of the persevering through force of nature to motivate, captivate, and interface us to the significant rhythms of the earth.

1.3 Introduce the main characters and their connection to Majestic Heights.

In the midst of the stunning scenes of Superb Levels, a cast of characters unfurls, each woven into the texture of this charming domain in exceptional and convincing ways. These people, attracted to Grand Levels because of reasons as different as the actual environment, become the channels through which the account of this dynamic locale unfurls.

At the core of this story is Emily Harper, a gutsy natural life moderate whose enthusiasm for safeguarding the rich biodiversity of Grand Levels characterizes her reality. With her khaki clothing and an endured cap safeguarding her from the African sun, Emily travels through the scene with an elegance that gives a false representation of her assurance. Having committed her life to understanding and safeguarding the different cluster of species that call Great Levels home, Emily is a residing demonstration of the harmonious connection among humankind and the regular world.

Her association with Superb Levels is well established, tracing all the way back to her young life when her folks, famous biologists, led historic exploration on the district's greenery. Growing up in the midst of the untamed magnificence of Glorious Levels, Emily fostered a significant love for the land, its animals, and the great Kilimanjaro that lingered not too far off. Her folks' heritage, scratched in the chronicles of natural science, energizes Emily's obligation to safeguarding the sensitive equilibrium of Magnificent Levels.

In the core of Magnificent Levels, Emily's way meets with that of Dr. Samuel Ngugi, a recognized geologist whose skill lies in the land miracles of Kilimanjaro. With a salt-and-pepper facial hair growth that clues at a long period of investigation and revelation, Dr. Ngugi is a researcher whose association with Glorious Levels rises above the scholar. He is driven by an oddity to disentangle the secrets of Kilimanjaro, from its land history to the unpretentious changes in its grand glacial masses.

Dr. Ngugi's excursion to Superb Levels started as a youthful scientist interested by the geographical wonders that lay secret inside Kilimanjaro's slants. Throughout the long term, his interest developed into a firmly established association with the mountain, where each rock arrangement and cold development turned into a part in the story of Earth's development. His exploration not just adds to the logical comprehension of Kilimanjaro yet in addition frames a connection among him and the mountain that goes past the domain of the scholarly community.

Emily and Dr. Ngugi, their ways converging at the intersection of ecological preservation and topographical investigation, end up joined by a common vision for the fate of Grand Levels. Together, they team up on drives that intend to blend human home with the safeguarding of the area's regular miracles. The cooperative energy between Emily's protection endeavors and Dr. Ngugi's land experiences makes a comprehensive way to deal with manageable living in Lofty Levels.

Amidst this coalition, a third person arises — Daniel Kiprop, a nearby craftsman whose material is the scene of Glorious Levels itself. With an easel set against the scenery of moving slopes and Kilimanjaro's outline, Daniel catches the embodiment of Glorious Levels with strokes of dynamic tones. His craft, a festival of the locale's excellence, fills in as a scaffold between the logical undertakings of Emily and Dr. Ngugi and the profound association that occupants and guests feel towards Superb Levels.

Daniel's foundations run somewhere down in Grand Levels, his predecessors having been stewards of the land for ages. His specialty isn't simply a portrayal of the actual scene however a visual articulation of the otherworldly association that individuals of Magnificent Levels share with their current circumstance. Through his canvases, Daniel turns into a narrator, protecting the stories of Glorious Levels in a medium that rises above words.

As the existences of Emily, Dr. Ngugi, and Daniel become complicatedly laced, Lofty Levels takes on new aspects. The moderate, the geologist, and the craftsman team up on projects that meld logical comprehension with profound reverberation. Emily's drives to safeguard natural life territories are supplemented by Dr. Ngugi's examination, which divulges the land establishments that support the environment. Daniel's craft, showed in collective spaces and displays across Superb Levels, turns into a social standard that develops the association among occupants and the land they possess.

In the midst of this triplet, a fourth person, Sarah Malik, arises — another occupant attracted to Lofty Levels by a longing for a groundbreaking valuable encounter. Sarah, a corporate leader looking for reprieve from the metropolitan hustle, tracks down comfort in the hug of Glorious Levels. Her process is one of rediscovery, as she submerges herself locally produced by Emily, Dr. Ngugi, and Daniel.

Sarah's association with Great Levels is more private than she at first understands. Unbeknownst to her, her family's foundations follow back to the native networks that have occupied Magnificent Levels for a really long time. As she reveals the layers of her genealogical legacy, Sarah turns into a connection between the past and the present, her presence representing the progression of life in Superb Levels.

The account unfurls as these characters explore the difficulties and wins that life in Grand Levels presents. Emily's protection endeavors face hindrances, from poaching dangers to the infringement of urbanization. Dr. Ngugi's topographical examinations reveal unpretentious changes in Kilimanjaro's scene, provoking reflections on the fragile harmony between human exercises and the world's normal cycles. Daniel's craft turns into an impetus for local area commitment, cultivating an aggregate pride in Lofty Levels' rich social and natural legacy.

As the characters' accounts interweave, Grand Levels itself turns into a person — a no nonsense substance that answers the activities and choices of its occupants. The scene, the natural life, and the transcending presence of Kilimanjaro are not simple settings but rather dynamic members in the account. Great Levels, through its different characters, turns into a microcosm of the sensitive dance among mankind and the regular world, a demonstration of the interconnectedness of all life.

In the last venture of this story, the characters wrestle with the always developing difficulties that defy Great Levels. A source of inspiration resounds through the slopes as the local area rallies to shield the district from outer dangers and to fashion a reasonable future. Emily, Dr. Ngugi, Daniel, and Sarah, each contributing their special assets, become the modelers of a heritage that will reverberate through the ages.

Lofty Levels, through the excursions of these characters, arises as a geological area as well as a representation for the aggregate human experience. It is where energy, interest, inventiveness, and familial ties combine to make a story that rises above the limits of reality. In the tremendous embroidery of Great Levels, the characters find a home as well as a material whereupon the story of their lives unfurls, everlastingly entwined with the untamed magnificence of this made up domain.

In the midst of the undulating magnificence of Glorious Levels, a group of four of characters winds around a rich embroidery of associations, every individual personally weaved with the scene, untamed life, and the transcending presence of Kilimanjaro.

These characters — Emily Harper, Dr. Samuel Ngugi, Daniel Kiprop, and Sarah Malik — typify different foundations, desires, and points of view, on the whole adding to the story of this charming domain.

Emily Harper, a dedicated untamed life protectionist, embodies the harmonious connection among humankind and nature in Glorious Levels. Her association with this enamoring area is well established in familial history. Emily's folks, recognized environmentalists, set out on historic examination inside the bounds of Glorious Levels, disentangling the complexities of its biological systems. Raised in the midst of the untamed excellence of this scene, Emily guzzled a love for the land, its animals, and the glorious Kilimanjaro that remained as a sentinel not too far off.

Lofty Levels, for Emily, isn't simply a working environment; a safehaven molded her perspective. Her cherished, lifelong recollections are carved against the setting of clearing slopes, flowing waterways, and the notable outline of Kilimanjaro. These developmental encounters developed an enthusiasm for preservation, moving her to commit her life to the insurance of Grand Levels' rich biodiversity. Emily's responsibility reaches out past logical meticulousness; a close to home tie to a spot addresses the sensitive harmony between human life and the regular world.

In the story embroidered artwork of Great Levels, Dr. Samuel Ngugi arises as a recognized geologist whose mastery digs into the topographical marvels of Kilimanjaro. A researcher with a salt-and-pepper facial hair growth and eyes that reflect the profundities of his geographical requests, Dr. Ngugi's association with Magnificent Levels is both scholarly and otherworldly. His interest with the land wonders of Kilimanjaro started in his childhood, filled by an oddity that developed into a long lasting excursion of investigation.

For Dr. Ngugi, the charm of Glorious Levels lies in the perplexing layers of Kilimanjaro's topographical history. His exploration, traversing many years, divulges the antiquated insider facts concealed inside the mountain's inclines, from the structure of its stones to the elements of its ice sheets. The geographical miracles of Kilimanjaro are not simply logical riddles for Dr. Ngugi; they are consecrated sections in the tale of Earth's development. His association with Great Levels rises above the scholastic domain, turning into a significant investigation of the transaction between the world's powers and the living biological system that flourishes at its base.

Converging these logical pursuits is Daniel Kiprop, a nearby craftsman whose material reaches out past traditional limits. With an easel set against the huge breadth of Glorious Levels, Daniel's craft turns into a visual festival of the scene, the natural life, and the profound pith of the district. His association with Magnificent Levels is well established in tribal ties, as his family has been stewards of the land for ages.

Daniel's specialty is certainly not a simple portrayal; a profound course spans the logical undertakings of Emily and Dr. Ngugi with the instinctive, social association that inhabitants and guests share with Superb Levels. Through his works of art, Daniel typifies the immaterial — the feelings mixed by the play of daylight on Kilimanjaro's icy masses, the dance of natural life across the fields, and the murmured accounts of Lofty Levels' native networks. His specialty turns into an impression of the spirit of Glorious Levels, a medium through which the scene addresses the hearts of the people who experience it.

As these three characters cross the interconnected domains of science, protection, and craftsmanship, another occupant, Sarah Malik, arises as a crucial figure in the story. A corporate leader looking for relief from the metropolitan tumult, Sarah's excursion to Glorious Levels is one of rediscovery and change. Unbeknownst to her, the foundations of her family reach out into the native networks that have flourished in Grand Levels for quite a long time.

Sarah's association with Magnificent Levels is at first fortunate, however as she dives into her family ancestry, it develops into a significant recovery of familial ties. Her process turns into a demonstration of the congruity of life in Glorious Levels, connecting the past with the present and encapsulating the repeating idea of presence in this captivating locale. Sarah's appearance implies more than individual disclosure; it represents the persevering through associations that people manufacture with Great Levels, no matter what their experiences or beginnings.

The group of four's connections and coordinated efforts inside Great Levels structure a story mosaic that reflects the variety and interconnectedness of the actual locale. Emily's preservation endeavors,

Dr. Ngugi's land requests, and Daniel's imaginative articulations join to make an all encompassing way to deal with maintainability. Their undertakings are not disconnected pursuits but rather strings in an embroidery that outlines the fragile dance between human exercises and the regular cycles of Glorious Levels.

As these characters explore the difficulties introduced by their individual reasons for living, Magnificent Levels goes through changes that mirror the consistently developing connection among mankind and the climate. Emily battles with the dangers presented by poaching and urbanization, Dr. Ngugi disentangles unpretentious changes in Kilimanjaro's geographical cosmetics, and Daniel's craft turns into an impetus for local area commitment. Sarah, as she continued looking for self-disclosure, turns into an extension between the familial tradition of Lofty Levels and the contemporary local area that occupies it.

The group of four's accounts are not simply individual stories; they are interconnected parts in the bigger adventure of Grand Levels. Together, they face outer dangers, fashion coalitions with the local area, and become overseers of a heritage that reaches out past their lifetimes. Glorious Levels, through the characters' aggregate undertakings, arises as a no nonsense substance — a biological system of human associations, social legacy, and regular miracles.

In the last venture of this story, a source of inspiration reverberations through the slopes of Lofty Levels. The people group rallies to shield the locale from outside dangers and to outline a reasonable future. Emily, Dr. Ngugi, Daniel, and Sarah, each contributing their extraordinary assets, become draftsmen of an inheritance that rises above the limits of time. The group of four typifies the soul of Magnificent Levels — where enthusiasm, interest, inventiveness, and tribal ties join to make a story that reverberates through the ages, everlastingly interlaced with the untamed magnificence of this imaginary domain.

Chapter 2

The Enigmatic Mountain

High in the distant districts of the Himalayas, covered in fog and secret, there lies a mountain that has caught the creative mind of pilgrims and spiritualists the same for quite a long time. Known by different names among various societies, this confounding pinnacle has been the subject of incalculable legends, fantasies, and murmured stories went down through ages.

Local people, shrewd and endured by the cruel states of their sloping home, discuss the top with a quieted veneration. To them, it is something beyond a geological component; it is a living element, a god that watches over their town with considerate eyes. They recount old ceremonies performed at the foundation of the mountain to conciliate its spirits, guaranteeing favorable luck and insurance for their local area.

As expression of the mountain's strange quality spread past the separated towns settled in the folds of the powerful reach, explorers and searchers of the obscure were attracted to its attractive force. The charm of neglected levels and untold mysteries implanted in the core of the mountain demonstrated compelling to those with a hunger for disclosure.

The excursion to the mountain was no simple accomplishment. The tough territory, misleading precipices, and flighty weather conditions made the climb an imposing test. However, for the individuals who thought about wandering into the obscure, the commitment of disentangling the mountain's mysteries merited the gamble. Numerous undertakings set out, furnished with the most recent innovation and directed by the insight of neighborhood Sherpas who had a personal information on the mountain's flighty demeanor.

The principal archived endeavor to vanquish the mountain was driven by the valiant pioneer, Sir Edmund Harrington, in the late nineteenth 100 years. Harrington, energized by the soul of the period of investigation, gathered a group of prepared mountain dwellers and left on a risky excursion to arrive at the highest point. Their records, protected in endured diaries and blurred photos, recount the difficulties they confronted - frostbite, torrential slides, and the always present danger of height disorder.

Notwithstanding their bold endeavors, Harrington and his group missed the mark concerning arriving at the tricky highest point. The mountain, it appeared, enviously protected its mysteries, opposing the interruption of human presence. Resolute, resulting endeavors continued in the years that followed, every one driven by the appeal of vanquishing the unconquerable.

In the mid twentieth hundred years, the confounding mountain turned into the focal point of logical request. Driven by a craving to comprehend the geographical and ecological secrets covered inside its transcending mass, scientists and geologists left on campaigns outfitted with cutting edge instruments. Their discoveries uncovered a perplexing biological system flourishing at heights that appeared to be ungracious to life.

Interesting and versatile greenery gripped to the sheer stone appearances, resisting the unforgiving circumstances. Creatures adjusted to the flimsy air and gnawing cold wandered the high-elevation levels, their endurance a demonstration of the mountain's exceptional biology. The scientists wondered about the sensitive equilibrium that permitted life to thrive in such outrageous circumstances, and their disclosures started another flood of interest in the mountain's mysteries.

As the twentieth century advanced, the mountain became an image of success as well as a reference point for profound searchers. Yogis, priests, and spiritualists from different practices looked for comfort and edification in the isolation of its slants. Legends discussed antiquated religious communities concealed in the folds of the mountain, where astute sages reflected in detachment, their psyches sensitive to the vast energies that pervaded the hallowed space.

The mountain, it appeared, held the way to opening a more profound comprehension of the universe and the interconnectedness, everything being equal. The people who wandered into its presence talked about dreams and supernatural encounters that opposed sane clarification.

The lines between the material and the powerful obscured, and the mountain turned into a scaffold between the natural domain and the ethereal unexplored world.

In the last 50% of the twentieth 100 years, headways in innovation achieved another period of investigation. Satellite symbolism, high level planning procedures, and specific climbing gear took into account more exact preparation and execution of campaigns. Yet again the competition to vanquish the most noteworthy tops on Earth heightened, and the confounding mountain wound up at the focal point of consideration.

Campaigns became worldwide undertakings, with climbers and researchers from various corners of the globe uniting in the mission to arrive at the culmination. The difficulties, nonetheless, stayed considerable. The mountain's capricious climate, sheer bluffs, and precipices tried the restrictions of human perseverance. Misfortunes struck, and lives were lost, as the quest for vanquishing the pinnacle demanded a weighty cost.

Regardless of the difficulties, the appeal of the cryptic mountain endured. It turned into an image of human versatility and assurance, a demonstration of the unstoppable soul that drove people to push the limits of what was considered conceivable. The mountain, it appeared, held a mirror to the human spirit, reflecting the two its solidarity and weakness.

In the 21st hundred years, the mountain entered another period of investigation as advances in computer generated simulation permitted easy chair swashbucklers to encounter the rising from the solace of their homes. Virtual undertakings, directed by experienced climbers and described via prepared mountain dwellers, gave a brief look into the difficulties and marvels of the excursion. The computerized domain opened up additional opportunities for investigation, permitting a worldwide crowd to interface with the persona of the baffling mountain.

However, even in the period of virtual investigation, the charm of the substantial, the smell of fresh mountain air, the mash of snow underneath, and the amazing vistas that extended as should have been obvious, stayed unrivaled. The call of the mountain kept on coaxing the individuals who looked for an immediate experience with its highness.

In the current day, the mountain remains as an image of both stunningness and modesty. It has seen the persistent quest for victory, the tranquil examination of spiritualists, and the logical investigation of specialists. It stays a conundrum, its insider facts monitored by the cold breezes that scope across tops and the old spirits are said to abide inside its rough heart.

The encompassing towns, unaltered by the progression of time, keep on giving recognition to the mountain with customs and services went down through ages. The mountain, thus, watches over them with an immortal look, a quiet gatekeeper that rises above the transient worries of the world underneath.

As the sun sets behind the transcending tops, providing reason to feel ambiguous about a brilliant sparkle the snow-covered culminations, the baffling mountain stays a reference point of secret, welcoming the inquisitive and the gutsy to leave on an excursion of disclosure. Whether through the actual afflictions of a rising, the reflective contemplation of a searcher, or the virtual investigation of a computerized explorer, the mountain keeps on winding around its spell, attracting the individuals who set out to disentangle its puzzle into its immortal hug.

2.1 Explore the history and mystique surrounding Mount Kilimanjaro.

Settled in the core of East Africa, Mount Kilimanjaro remains as a magnificent sentinel, its snow-covered tops puncturing the sky. Ascending to a height of 19,341 feet (5,895 meters), Kilimanjaro is Africa's most elevated mountain and a signal for explorers and nature devotees from around the globe. Its transcending presence has molded the scene as well as woven an embroidery of history and persona that charms the individuals who try to investigate its slants.

The narrative of Mount Kilimanjaro starts ages back, as volcanic movement formed the East African Fracture Framework, leading to this notorious pinnacle. The mountain is a stratovolcano made out of three cones: Kibo, Mawenzi, and Shira. While Shira is torpid, Kibo — the most elevated culmination — houses the stunning Uhuru Pinnacle, an objective that has filled the fantasies of courageous wayfarers for a really long time.

Well before the primary recorded rising, Kilimanjaro held a position of importance in the convictions and customs of the native individuals who possessed the encompassing grounds. The Chaga public, who have called the lower regions of Kilimanjaro home for quite a long time, instilled the mountain with otherworldly significance. They accepted that the snow on its highest point addressed immaculateness and holiness, and stories of mysterious animals abiding in its shadows reverberated through their oral practices.

The main archived European locating of Kilimanjaro is ascribed to the German evangelist Johannes Rebmann during the nineteenth 100 years. His records of a snow-covered mountain close to the equator were at first met with doubt in Europe, as it tested the common conviction that such a peculiarity was unthinkable in the African jungles.

Rebmann's reports, in any case, provoked the curiosity of travelers and lighted a longing to unwind the secrets hid inside the core of Africa.

The late nineteenth and mid twentieth hundreds of years saw a flood in investigation, as European swashbucklers and mountain climbers put their focus on the immaculate domains of the world. Kilimanjaro, with its charming snow-clad pinnacle, turned into an image of the unknown and the extraordinary. The competition to overcome levels reflected the more extensive soul of investigation characterized the period.

The principal effective climb of Kilimanjaro is credited to Hans Meyer, a German geologist, and Ludwig Purtscheller, an Austrian mountain climber, in 1889. Their campaign, loaded with difficulties and difficulties, denoted a noteworthy second as they arrived at the highest point of Uhuru Top on October 6, 1889. Meyer's record of the rising, loaded up with portrayals of the remarkable scene and the actual afflictions of the ascension, carried Kilimanjaro into the worldwide awareness.

As fresh insight about the effective rising spread, Kilimanjaro failed to be a simple geological component and changed into an image of human accomplishment. The mountain, when covered in secret, presently turned into an objective for those looking to test their grit against the powers of nature. The appeal of remaining on the top of Africa, looking across the tremendous savannah underneath, drew swashbucklers and mountain dwellers from various corners of the world.

The encompassing district, with its different biological systems and interesting widely varied vegetation, added to Kilimanjaro's allure. The mountain's inclines are a microcosm of climatic zones, from lavish rainforests to snow capped knolls, giving an environment to a rich cluster of plant and creature life. The trip to the culmination turned into an excursion through these biological zones, offering climbers an uncommon chance to observe the stunning variety of East Africa in a solitary rising.

Kilimanjaro's persona stretches out past its actual glory. The native individuals, with their profound association with the mountain, have woven legends and customs around its slants. Legends talk about hereditary spirits dwelling in its rough hole, and ceremonies are performed to pacify these watchmen of the mountain. Kilimanjaro, to the Chaga public, is a living substance, its prosperity entwined with the destiny of the encompassing networks.

The profound meaning of Kilimanjaro isn't bound to neighborhood convictions alone. In ongoing many years, searchers of profound illumination and comprehensive prosperity have been attracted to the mountain. The quiet scenes and the significant quietness that encompasses the higher compasses of Kilimanjaro make an air helpful for reflection and contemplation. Yogis, careful voyagers, and those looking for inward harmony track down comfort in the serene hug of the mountain.

Deductively, Kilimanjaro has been a subject of study for scientists trying to comprehend the effects of environmental change. The contracting ice sheets on its highest point have turned into a noticeable marker of ecological movements, inciting worries about the drawn out supportability of this famous scene. The sensitive harmony between the regular excellence of Kilimanjaro and the natural difficulties it faces highlights the requirement for worldwide protection endeavors.

In the domain of writing and mainstream society, Kilimanjaro has made a permanent imprint. Ernest Hemingway's brief tale "The Snows of Kilimanjaro" deified the mountain in the abstract group. Hemingway, who visited East Africa during the 1930s, drew motivation from Kilimanjaro's icy masses and the encompassing scenes to create a story of disappointment, reflection, and the transitory idea of life.

In the story, the hero, lying on his deathbed on the slants of Kilimanjaro, ponders the unfulfilled dreams and botched open doors that characterize his life. Hemingway's reminiscent composition catches the substance of Kilimanjaro as a geological milestone as well as a similitude for the transient idea of human life. The snows of Kilimanjaro, immaculate by time, act as a strong setting to the hero's introspections.

Kilimanjaro's impact stretches out to the universe of film too. Movie producers have been attracted to its emotional scenes, involving the mountain as a scenery for experience stories, narratives, and fictitious stories. The visual appeal of Kilimanjaro, with its broad vistas and tough landscape, has graced the cinema, further implanting its picture in the aggregate creative mind.

In the 21st 100 years, Kilimanjaro keeps on alluring globe-trotters, adventurers, and nature fans. The notoriety of climbing endeavors has taken off, with different courses taking care of various expertise levels and inclinations. The Machame Course, known for its dazzling view, and the Marangu Course, frequently alluded to as the "Coca-Cola Course," are among the most visited ways to the culmination.

Climbing Kilimanjaro isn't without its difficulties. The height, outrageous weather patterns, and actual requests make it a long term hardship and assurance. Acclimatization turns into a urgent part of the rising, as climbers explore through the different environmental zones, acclimating to the evolving heights.

The fellowship manufactured on the inclines of Kilimanjaro is a demonstration of the common human experience of beating difficulties. Climbers from various corners of the world, associated by a shared objective, structure bonds as they rise towards the highest point. The feeling of achievement after arriving at Uhuru Pinnacle isn't just an individual victory however a festival of the aggregate soul that characterizes the human journey for investigation.

As Kilimanjaro keeps on drawing individuals from different foundations, the significance of capable the travel industry and protection turns out to be progressively clear. Endeavors to safeguard the natural respectability of the mountain, diminish the ecological impression of climbers, and backing nearby networks are indispensable to guaranteeing that Kilimanjaro's heritage perseveres for people in the future.

All in all, the set of experiences and persona encompassing Mount Kilimanjaro are woven into the texture of human investigation, profound looking for, and natural mindfulness. From its beginnings as a geographical wonder to its change into an image of human accomplishment, Kilimanjaro has remained as a quiet observer to the recurring pattern of time.

As climbers stand on the highest point, looking across the tremendous scope beneath, they become piece of a continuum that traverses ages. Kilimanjaro, with its quiet grandness, helps us to remember the interconnectedness of the regular world and the human soul. Whether seen as an actual test, a profound journey, or a material for imaginative articulation, Kilimanjaro keeps on rousing wonderment and worship, welcoming all who experience it to turn out to be essential for its getting through story.

2.2 Delve into the local legends and myths that have been passed down through generations.

In the calm corners of the world, where customs are woven into the texture of day to day existence, nearby legends and fantasies flourish as narrators pass down stories starting with one age then onto the next. These stories, wealthy in social importance, give a window into the aggregate creative mind of networks, offering bits of knowledge into their convictions, fears, and values. As we dive into the domains of these neighborhood legends, we wind up moved to an existence where the limit among the real world and the otherworldly hazy spots, leading to charming stories that persevere through time.

One such district saturated with legend and secret is the Scottish Good countries, where jagged mountains and fog covered lochs give a frightful setting to old stories. Among the numerous legends that reverberation through the glens, the tale of the Loch Ness Beast stands apart as a demonstration of the getting through charm of legendary animals. Nessie, as the animal is lovingly known, is said to possess the dull waters of Loch Ness, a serpentine lake that stretches for a significant distance.

The starting points of the Loch Ness Beast fantasy can be followed back to old Celtic fables, where water spirits were accepted to possess the lochs and streams. In any case, it was only after the twentieth century that Nessie caught the world's creative mind. In 1933, a couple professed to have seen a huge, ancient animal rising up out of the profundities of Loch Ness. The locating ignited a whirlwind of premium, and from that point forward, endless records of Nessie sightings have been accounted for.

Notwithstanding broad logical examinations and innovative headways, the secret of the Loch Ness Beast perseveres. Whether a flesh animal or a fantasy of aggregate creative mind, Nessie stays an indispensable piece of High country legends, enamoring the personalities of local people and guests the same. The legend of the Loch Ness Beast addresses mankind's interest with the obscure and the getting through force of fantasy to shape our view of the normal world.

Going across the globe to the fog covered scenes of Japan, we experience the legendary animal known as the kappa. In Japanese fables, the kappa is a water demon that possesses streams and lakes. Portrayed as a humanoid animal with a dish-like sorrow on head holds water, the kappa is both naughty and possibly perilous. It is said that in the event that one bows to a kappa, the animal will bow consequently, making the water in its mind spill, delivering it feeble.

The kappa isn't only a wake up call; it fills in as a social image, epitomizing the regard and worship for nature. In antiquated times, individuals living in agrarian networks were exceptionally reliant upon water hotspots for their occupations. The kappa, with its relationship with water, turned into a figurative gatekeeper of streams and an indication of the sensitive harmony among people and the normal world.

Similarly as with numerous legendary animals, the kappa's depiction fluctuates across areas, with nearby subtleties forming the story. In spite of its extraordinary properties, the kappa mirrors the advantageous connection among people and nature in Japanese old stories, featuring the significance of conjunction and shared regard.

Wandering into the core of Africa, we experience the rich embroidery of fantasies woven by different societies. In the Yoruba folklore of Nigeria, Olokun, the goddess of the ocean, holds a position of respect. Olokun is accepted to live in the profundities of the sea, using control over the immense breadth of water. Her folklore is interwoven with topics of creation, overflow, and the secrets of the ocean.

The Yoruba public, with their profound association with the regular world, view Olokun as a big-hearted god who gives endowments to the individuals who honor her. Customs and services are directed to give proper respect to Olokun, looking for her approval for abundant harvests and insurance from the erratic powers of the ocean. The folklore of Olokun mirrors the Yoruba nation's amicable relationship with the climate, recognizing the powers unchangeable as far as they might be concerned while looking for agreement with the heavenly.

In the extensive deserts of the Center East, the Bedouin Evenings stories transport us to a domain of wizardry and charm. Perhaps of the most famous figure in these accounts is the unbelievable Aladdin, a young fellow who coincidentally finds a mystical light containing a strong genie. The story, woven into the assortment of stories known as "1,000 and One Evenings," has enraptured crowds for a really long time.

Aladdin's experiences, set against the scenery of a fictionalized Center Eastern city, take him from destitution to riches, with the genie conceding him wishes that change the direction of his life. The tale of Aladdin is in excess of a fantastical story; it mirrors the social creative mind of the Bedouin world, with its lively markets, otherworldly scenes, and the immortal subject of wishes satisfied through the mediation of mysterious creatures.

The persevering through allure of Aladdin's story lies in its widespread subjects of desire, change, and the acknowledgment of dreams. The story has risen above its social beginnings to turn into a worldwide image of the force of creative mind and the quest for a superior life.

Turning our look to the native people groups of North America, we experience the fantasy of the Thunderbird — a strong and superb animal that shows up in the folklore of different Local American clans. The Thunderbird is many times portrayed as a monster bird with wings that length the sky, fit for making roar by fluttering its wings and projecting lightning with its eyes.

Among the Ojibwe public, the Thunderbird is a huge otherworldly substance related with tempests and the nurturing downpours they bring. The fantasy of the Thunderbird is entwined with the patterns of nature, underscoring the interconnectedness of every living thing and the significance of keeping up with offset with the normal world.

Across various clans, varieties of the Thunderbird fantasy exist, each mirroring the one of a kind viewpoints and encounters of the native people groups. The Thunderbird fills in as an image of otherworldly power, a sign of the holy binds that tight spot mankind to the earth, sky, and waters.

In the foggy good countries of Papua New Guinea, the Asaro Mudmen encapsulate a living legend that has captivated anthropologists and explorers the same. The Asaro public, living in the Eastern Good countries, have a custom of wearing elaborate mud veils and earth covered bodies, giving them an extraordinary appearance. As per neighborhood legend, the Mudmen began from a town that was gone after by a foe clan.

Supposedly, the enduring individuals from the went after town looked for shelter in a stream, covering themselves in mud to stow away. At the point when they rose up out of the water, their mud-covered bodies and alarming veils terrified away their adversaries. The legend of the Mudmen has been gone down through ages, and the practice of the Asaro Mudmen proceeds right up to the present day, filling in as a social articulation that obscures the lines among the real world and fantasy.

The act of the Mudmen mirrors the flexibility and innovativeness of the Asaro public, who changed a verifiable occasion into a living legend that shapes their social personality. The Mudmen custom is a demonstration of the getting through force of narrating, permitting networks to reconsider and reevaluate their stories across time.

These brief looks into nearby legends and fantasies from various corners of the world uncover the all inclusive human motivation to look for significance and grasping through narrating. Whether established in nature, history, or the heavenly, fantasies act as a social mirror, mirroring the qualities, fears, and yearnings of networks.

As we explore the embroidery of worldwide legends, we track down ongoing ideas that tight spot humankind — a veneration for the normal world, an interest with the obscure, and a longing to figure out the secrets that shape our reality. Neighborhood legends and fantasies, with their immortal stories, welcome us to leave on an excursion of creative mind, interfacing us to the aggregate insight of societies across existence.

2.3 Introduce the concept of Kilimanjaro's secrets and the intrigue surrounding the mountain.

In the immense scope of East Africa, where the general savannah meets the sky, a singular monster rises, creating its shaded area across the land. Mount Kilimanjaro, with its snow-covered tops and tough inclines, remains as a sentinel of secret and charm. Past its actual magnificence, Kilimanjaro harbors mysteries that have captivated wayfarers, researchers, and spiritualists for a really long time. As we disentangle the layers of Kilimanjaro's insider facts, we enter a domain where the substantial and the ethereal combine, welcoming us to mull over the puzzler that covers this famous mountain.

The interest encompassing Kilimanjaro isn't exclusively established in its transcending level or dazzling vistas. It lies in the layers of history, culture, and normal miracle that have gathered after some time, making an embroidery of mysteries that coaxes the people who look to figure out the mountain's substance.

At the core of Kilimanjaro's persona is the love it orders among the native individuals who call its lower regions home. The Chaga public, with their profound association with the land, view Kilimanjaro not just as a geological element but rather as a consecrated substance, a residence of spirits and familial energies. Legends went down through ages talk about customs performed at the mountain's base to respect these concealed powers and secure the prosperity of the encompassing networks.

The actual soil of Kilimanjaro, rich and ripe, tells a story of patterns of life and demise. The mountain's slants, embellished with different biological systems going from lavish rainforests to infertile high deserts, act as a living material painted with the brushstrokes of development. Each plant, every animal that calls Kilimanjaro home, adds to the mind boggling snare of life, adding to the privileged insights woven into the texture of the mountain.

Logical investigation has stripped back certain layers of Kilimanjaro's secrets. Analysts, drawn by the novel environmental variety of the mountain, have wandered into its folds to open the mysteries of its vegetation. Uncommon and strong species, adjusted to the brutal states of high heights, have been found sticking to rough cleft and flourishing in apparently unfriendly conditions. Kilimanjaro, it shows up, isn't simply a transcending top however a safe-haven for life that overcomes customary presumption.

However, as science reveals insight into the natural miracles of Kilimanjaro, it at the same time develops the secret encompassing its contracting ice sheets. The famous ice cap that crowns the highest point, when an image of timeless excellence, is subsiding at a disturbing rate — an obvious sign of the worldwide effects of environmental change. The privileged insights concealed inside Kilimanjaro's ice resemble antiquated compositions, gradually softening endlessly, conveying with them pieces of information to the mountain's past and alerts for its future.

The appeal of Kilimanjaro reaches out past the logical domain. Globe-trotters and mountain climbers, drawn by the test of vanquishing its levels, set out on misleading excursions that stretch the boundaries of human perseverance. The mountain, with its capricious climate, sheer bluffs, and slender air, turns into a cauldron where the unyielding soul of humankind is tried. The narratives of win and misfortune that reverberation through Kilimanjaro's slants add a layer of human show to the mountain's privileged insights, a demonstration of the strength and weakness of the people who set out to wander into the unexplored world.

In the records of investigation, Kilimanjaro plays had a focal impact, drawing in trailblazers and visionaries who tried to unwind its secrets. Sir Edmund Harrington's notable endeavor to vanquish the mountain in the late nineteenth century denoted the start of another part in Kilimanjaro's story. The stories of early undertakings, with their battles against frostbite, torrential slides, and the tireless powers of nature, highlighted the impressive difficulties that Kilimanjaro introduced to the individuals who looked to arrive at its culmination.

As innovation progressed, Kilimanjaro turned into the focal point of logical request. Geologists, outfitted with instruments to test the mountain's privileged insights, dove into its land history, unwinding the secrets of its development. The stones and residue that make up Kilimanjaro's design turned into a period case, safeguarding pieces of information about the old powers that molded the scene.

However, notwithstanding the steps in logical comprehension, Kilimanjaro stays where the experimental and the mysterious converge. The neighborhood guides, who explore the slippery territory with a closeness brought into the world of ages, discuss the mountain as a living substance with temperaments and spirits of its own. The old stories of the Chaga public, interlaced with the rhythms of the normal world, murmurs of stowed away domains inside Kilimanjaro that evade the grip of logical examination.

The charm of Kilimanjaro isn't bound to the actual domain. Spiritualists and searchers, drawn by the mountain's otherworldly reverberation, adventure into its presence looking for greatness and edification. Kilimanjaro turns into a holy space, an edge where the natural and the heavenly unite. Dreams and encounters that challenge normal clarification are woven into the texture of Kilimanjaro's insider facts, welcoming the people who track slants to consider the secrets rise above the limits of the material world.

The conundrum of Kilimanjaro develops as we investigate the legends that have been gone down through ages. Nearby fantasies talk about antiquated cloisters concealed in the folds of the mountain, where shrewd sages contemplate in seclusion, their brains sensitive to the vast energies that pervade the holy space. These stories, gave over as oral practices, allude to aspects of Kilimanjaro's secrets that rise above the noticeable and substantial.

In the period of virtual investigation, Kilimanjaro takes on new aspects. Computer generated reality permits easy chair explorers to set out on advanced endeavors, directed by experienced climbers and described via prepared mountain climbers. The virtual rising, however without any trace of actual difficulties, catches the embodiment of Kilimanjaro's charm, offering a brief look into the insider facts that have drawn pioneers for a really long time.

The mysterious air of Kilimanjaro reaches out past the domain of science and experience. It is a social standard, motivating craftsmen, essayists, and movie producers to catch its quintessence. The snows of Kilimanjaro, deified in writing by Ernest Hemingway, act as a similitude for the passing idea of life and the second thoughts that wait in the human spirit. The mountain turns into a material for realistic stories, a scenery for stories that investigate the human condition even with nature's highness.

Kilimanjaro's insider facts, similar to the layers of its transcending inclines, are diverse and subtle. They envelop the organic miracles of its environments, the topographical secrets of its arrangement, the social importance implanted in neighborhood customs, and the profound aspects that rise above the material world. The mountain, with its frigid crown and quiet presence, welcomes us to consider the interconnectedness, all things considered, the fragile dance between the substantial and the immaterial.

All in all, Kilimanjaro stands as an actual milestone as well as a vault of mysteries that coax us to investigate, to address, and to wonder. Whether moved toward from the perspective of science, experience, otherworldliness, or craftsmanship, Kilimanjaro uncovers itself as a residing element, where the shroud between the known and the obscure is flimsy. As we explore its slants, we become piece of an immortal story, one that rises above the limits of geology and coaxes us to reveal the mysteries that untruth concealed inside the core of this notorious mountain.

In the core of East Africa, where the rambling savannas meet the tremendous skies, a transcending sentinel of secret and grandness rises — the famous Mount Kilimanjaro. Past its actual unmistakable quality, Kilimanjaro is covered in a riddle that has enamored travelers, researchers, and visionaries for a really long time. The interest encompassing the mountain is an intricate embroidery woven with strings of history, culture, science, and the ethereal, making a story that rises above the unmistakable limits of its transcending inclines.

The charm of Kilimanjaro starts with the native people groups who have long occupied the lower regions of the mountain. The Chaga public, with their well established association with the land, don't only consider Kilimanjaro to be a geological element; they view it as a consecrated substance, a store of spirits and hereditary energies. Legends went down through ages discuss ceremonies directed at the mountain's base, an emblematic demonstration of regarding the inconspicuous powers that oversee the district and guaranteeing the success and security of their networks.

Kilimanjaro, according to the Chaga, is in excess of a geographical development; it is a living element with its own rhythms and temperaments. The mountain turns into an otherworldly anchor, a wellspring of solidarity and comfort for the people who stay in its shadow. As the Chaga mesh their old stories into the texture of Kilimanjaro, the mountain changes from an actual presence to a representative power that shapes their perspective and social personality.

Logical investigation has added layers to the interest encompassing Kilimanjaro. Scientists, drawn by the natural miracles of the mountain, have dove into its different biological systems, concentrating on the uncommon and versatile widely varied vegetation that have adjusted to its shifting elevations. Kilimanjaro, with its rainforests, snow capped glades, and fruitless pinnacles, turns into a microcosm of life's diligence notwithstanding testing conditions. The mountain's privileged insights, concealed inside its environmental variety, uncover the complexities of nature's capacity to flourish despite everything.

However, as science enlightens specific parts of Kilimanjaro's secrets, it all the while extends the secret encompassing its contracting icy masses. The notable ice cap that crowns the highest point, when a timeless image of magnificence, is subsiding at a disturbing rate — a distinct indication of the worldwide effects of environmental change. The insider facts installed inside Kilimanjaro's ice, similar to antiquated compositions, are gradually liquefying endlessly, conveying with them hints to the mountain's past and alerts for its future.

The appeal of Kilimanjaro reaches out past the logical domain to the domain of experience. The mountain, with its difficult territory, erratic climate, and slender air, has turned into a pot for travelers and mountain climbers. The craving to vanquish Kilimanjaro, to remain on its culmination and look across the huge scenes beneath, has drawn people from various corners of the world. The tales of win and misfortune that reverberation through Kilimanjaro's slants become piece of its living inheritance, meshing human show into the texture of its privileged insights.

Kilimanjaro's spot in the archives of investigation is huge. Sir Edmund Harrington's noteworthy endeavor to vanquish the mountain in the late nineteenth century denoted the start of another section in Kilimanjaro's story. The stories of early campaigns, full of battles against frostbite, torrential slides, and the tenacious powers of nature, highlight the considerable difficulties that Kilimanjaro introduced to the people who looked to arrive at its culmination.

As innovation progressed, Kilimanjaro turned into a point of convergence for logical request. Geologists, outfitted with instruments to test the mountain's insider facts, dug into its land history, unwinding the secrets of its development. The stones and silt that make up Kilimanjaro's design turned into a period container, saving pieces of information about the old powers that formed the scene.

However, notwithstanding the steps in logical comprehension, Kilimanjaro stays where the experimental and the enchanted converge. The nearby aides, who explore the misleading landscape with a closeness brought into the world of ages, discuss the mountain as a living substance with mind-sets and spirits of its own. The fables of the Chaga public, entwined with the rhythms of the regular world, murmurs of stowed away domains inside Kilimanjaro that escape the grip of logical investigation.

The appeal of Kilimanjaro isn't bound to the actual domain. Spiritualists and searchers, drawn by the mountain's profound reverberation, adventure into its presence looking for amazing quality and illumination. Kilimanjaro turns into a hallowed space, a limit where the natural and the heavenly join. Dreams and encounters that oppose reasonable clarification are woven into the texture of Kilimanjaro's privileged insights, welcoming the people who track inclines to ponder the secrets rise above the limits of the material world.

The puzzler of Kilimanjaro extends as we investigate the legends that have been gone down through ages. Nearby fantasies discuss antiquated cloisters concealed in the folds of the mountain, where savvy sages contemplate in separation, their psyches receptive to the astronomical energies that penetrate the sacrosanct space. These stories, gave over as oral customs, indicate aspects of Kilimanjaro's secrets that rise above the noticeable and substantial.

In the period of virtual investigation, Kilimanjaro takes on new aspects. Computer generated reality permits easy chair swashbucklers to set out on advanced campaigns, directed by experienced climbers and described via prepared mountain dwellers. The virtual rising, however without any trace of actual difficulties, catches the quintessence of Kilimanjaro's charm, offering a brief look into the privileged insights that have drawn voyagers for quite a long time.

The baffling emanation of Kilimanjaro reaches out past the domain of science and experience. It is a social standard, moving specialists, essayists, and movie producers to catch its quintessence. The snows of Kilimanjaro, deified in writing by Ernest Hemingway, act as a similitude for the transient idea of life and the second thoughts that wait in the human spirit. The mountain turns into a material for realistic stories, a setting for stories that investigate the human condition even with nature's highness.

Kilimanjaro's mysteries, similar to the layers of its transcending slants, are multi-layered and tricky. They envelop the natural miracles of its environments, the land secrets of its development, the social importance implanted in neighborhood customs, and the otherworldly aspects that rise above the material world. The mountain, with its frosty crown and quiet presence, welcomes us to ponder the interconnectedness, everything being equal, the sensitive dance between the unmistakable and the immaterial.

All in all, Kilimanjaro stands as an actual milestone as well as a store of mysteries that coax us to investigate, to address, and to wonder. Whether moved toward from the perspective of science, experience, otherworldliness, or workmanship, Kilimanjaro uncovers itself as a residing substance, where the shroud between the known and the obscure is slim. As we explore its slants, we become piece of an immortal story, one that rises above the limits of geology and entices us to reveal the mysteries that untruth concealed inside the core of this notorious mountain.

3

Chapter 3

The Protagonist's Arrival

In the curious town of Eldoria, settled between moving slopes and thick timberlands, the air hummed with a peculiar energy on the day the hero showed up. Eldoria had for some time been a shelter for those looking for comfort from the clamoring outside world, its cobbled roads and rural cabins shaping a pleasant scene of a less complex time.

As the hero's process unfurled, the residents really wanted to feel an unobtrusive change in the environment. It was as though the actual texture of Eldoria's world shuddered with expectation, mindful of a looming change. No one knew definitively why the hero had picked this distant town as their objective, yet destiny had woven its strings, carrying them to the limit of another experience.

The hero, a secretive figure shrouded in shadows, entered Eldoria with a calm assurance. Outsiders were a unique case in the town, and the occupants traded inquisitive looks as the newbie navigated the thin pathways. The air was thick with interest and implicit inquiries, and it appeared to be like the actual town paused its breathing.

Eldoria's senior, a savvy and endured man named Oryn, felt a significant association with the unfurling occasions. From his unassuming dwelling at the core of the town, Oryn detected that the hero's appearance proclaimed a urgent crossroads in Eldoria's set of experiences. The senior's sharp instinct had directed the town through innumerable difficulties, and presently, he remained on the cliff of one more conundrum.

As the hero wandered further into the core of Eldoria, they noticed the locals approaching their regular routines. Kids played close to the town well, their chuckling reverberating through the air, while experts carried out their specialties in curious studios. Eldoria radiated an immortal appeal, a safe-haven immaculate by the tenacious walk of progress.

The hero's presence didn't be ignored. Eldoria's occupants, consistently sensitive to the rhythmic movement of their affectionate local area, felt an implicit association with the outsider. Murmurs wandered through the town like a delicate breeze, conveying stories of the secretive figure who had passed the boundary into their quiet safe house.

As nightfall settled over Eldoria, the hero wound up attracted to the town square, where an endured stone wellspring remained as a quiet observer to the progression of time. The square filled in as the core of Eldoria, a space where locals accumulated to share stories, commend celebrations, and look for comfort in one another's organization.

A gathering of older folks, including Oryn, saw the hero's appearance in the square. With an aggregate gesture, they moved toward the baffling figure, their eyes mirroring a mix of interest and intelligence collected throughout the long term. Oryn, the senior, ventured forward, his voice conveying the heaviness of involvement.

"Welcome to Eldoria, stranger. We sense that your appearance is no simple fortuitous event," Oryn talked, his look puncturing through the shadows that hidden the hero.

The hero, quiet as of recently, recognized Oryn's words with an unobtrusive gesture. Obviously their process had carried them to Eldoria with a reason, a reason that would entwine with the fates of the residents.

Oryn, ever discerning, welcomed the hero to share their story by the fireside. Eldoria's elderly folks accumulated all around, their eyes fixed on the perplexing figure as the story unfurled. The hero's story wove an embroidery of far off lands, old predictions, and a journey that rose above the limits of time.

The residents tuned in careful focus, dazzled by the unfurling adventure that currently crossed with their peaceful lives. Eldoria, it appeared, was not only a sanctuary; it was a nexus where the strings of predetermination united.

As the hero talked, an acknowledgment unfolded upon Oryn and the older folks. The town, when a safe house in the outskirts of the world, was bound to assume a significant part in a grandiose show. Eldoria's destiny had become laced with the hero's journey, and the townspeople, purposely or unconsciously, were endowed with a job in the unfurling adventure.

In the days that followed, Eldoria hummed with a recently discovered energy. The locals, roused by the hero's excursion, started to see their curious environmental elements from an alternate perspective. The cobbled roads, once strolled with routine commonality, presently reverberated with the strides of the people who detected the flows of fate.

The hero, having shared their story, turned into an essential piece of Eldoria's people group. The locals, perceiving the meaning of the more interesting's mission, offered help and help. Craftsmans made devices and relics, ranchers gave food, and researchers dove into old texts to disentangle the secrets predicted in the hero's excursion.

Eldoria changed into a clamoring center point of movement, its rural appeal compared against the direness of the unfurling adventure. The hero, when a single explorer, presently remained in charge of an aggregate undertaking that rose above individual fates. Eldoria, it appeared, had turned into a pot where standard lives would be tempered into remarkable stories.

As the hero dug further into their journey, Eldoria's scenes turned into a scenery to a progression of preliminaries and disclosures. The thick timberlands that lined the town held onto old mysteries, and the moving slopes hid neglected ruins that murmured stories of former periods.

Oryn, the town senior, expected the job of an aide and tutor to the hero. His insight, saturated with the legend of Eldoria, turned into a compass in the strange domains of the journey. Together, they translated obscure engravings, explored tricky scenes, and looked for the guidance of otherworldly creatures who abided in the secret corners of the town.

The connection between the hero and Eldoria extended as time passes. The locals, when limited by the schedules of their basic lives, presently wound up piece of a fabulous story that unfurled like the pages of an old book. Eldoria's personality, when characterized by its immortal appeal, extended to embrace the reverberations of vast powers that resonated through its actual soil.

In the core of Eldoria, a holy woods remained as a nexus between the unremarkable and the magical. It was here that the hero got dreams, brief looks at the past and future interweaved. The hallowed forest, washed in the ethereal sparkle of twilight, turned into a position of fellowship between the natural and the powerful.

As the hero advanced on their journey, Eldoria confronted its portion of difficulties. Dim powers, drawn by the hero's excursion, looked to disentangle the fragile equilibrium that the town addressed. Shadows crawled into the town square, murmurs of vindictive purpose saturating the hearts of those vulnerable to the appeal of force.

Eldoria's solidarity was tried, yet the locals, motivated by the hero's flexibility, stood firm. Bonds fashioned through shared preliminaries demonstrated solid, and the town turned into a stronghold against the infringing murkiness. Eldoria, when a quiet shelter, turned into an encouraging sign notwithstanding approaching shadows.

The hero, troubled by the heaviness of predetermination, tracked down comfort in Eldoria's hug. The town, thusly, drew strength from the hero's steadfast determination. The harmonious connection between the individual and the aggregate turned into a wellspring of strength that endured the preliminaries laid before them.

As the mission unfurled, Eldoria's scenes changed into a performance center of enchantment and secret. The thick woods, when seen as simple limits, uncovered entries to domains outside human ability to grasp. Eldoria's occupants, at first limited by the impediments of the unremarkable, found dormant capacities that rose above the standard.

The hero's process turned into a journey that reshaped Eldoria's actual quintessence. Old predictions, carved into the stones of the town square, spread out like parchments directed by an imperceptible hand. Eldoria, it appeared, was an embroidery woven with strings of destiny, and the hero's appearance was the impetus that unwound the enormous plan.

In the shadow of Eldoria's antiquated wellspring, the hero confronted their most considerable test. A combination of powers, both kindhearted and vindictive, appeared in a climactic conflict that reverberated through the town square. Oryn, the senior, remained by the hero's side, his insight a defense against the infringing whirlwind.

The fight unfurled with a fierceness that shook the actual groundworks of Eldoria. Esoteric energies impacted, and the air popped with the strain of contradicting powers. The residents, their countenances carved sincerely, remained as a unified front against the approaching obscurity that tried to inundate their shelter.

Amidst the disorder, the hero defied the encapsulation of the dull powers that tried to disentangle the texture of Eldoria. A figure shrouded in shadows, reflecting the hero's own outline, remained as the harbinger of conflict. The conflict among light and shadow played out like an enormous expressive dance, every development molding the fate of Eldoria.

Oryn, drawing upon the old information on Eldoria, diverted his insight into a defensive boundary that protected the town from the invasion of vindictive powers. The hero, engaged by the aggregate strength of Eldoria's occupants, confronted their doppelganger in a duel that rose above the actual domain.

The fight arrived at its pinnacle as the hero, with a flood of internal determination, vanquished the shadowy foe. The reverberations of the triumph resonated through Eldoria, dissipating the approaching dimness that had taken steps to obscure the town's light. The holy woods, when covered in vulnerability, sprouted with newly discovered essentialness.

With the equilibrium reestablished, Eldoria inhaled a deep breath of help. The locals, having confronted the pot of difficulty, arose more grounded and more associated than any time in recent memory. The hero, their mission satisfied, remained in the town square as an image of flexibility and win.

As Eldoria got back to its quiet beat, the hero detected the strings of predetermination unwinding. The town, when a nexus of grandiose powers, settled once more into the hug of its immortal appeal. The cobbled roads, observer to the new preliminaries, reverberated with the chuckling of kids and the murmur of day to day existence.

Oryn, the senior, moved toward the hero with a knowing grin. "Your presence has perpetually modified the woven artwork of Eldoria," he talked, his eyes mirroring the heaviness of the excursion they had shared. "Yet, as the flows of predetermination recurring pattern, the town will persevere, a signal for the individuals who look for shelter and reason."

The hero, their association with Eldoria carved in the records of time, bid goodbye to the town that had turned into a safe-haven and a pot. As they crossed the cobbled roads one last time, the reverberations of Eldoria's immortal appeal murmured stories of an excursion that rose above the limits of conventional lives.

Eldoria, having faced the hardship, remained as a demonstration of the cooperative dance between individual predetermination and aggregate versatility. The town, perpetually different by the hero's appearance, embraced the rhythmic movement of time, a sanctuary for the people who looked for comfort and reason in the delicate hug of its cobbled roads and provincial houses.

The hero's outline blurred into the distance, abandoning a town that had turned into a section in their journey. Eldoria, washed in the gleam of the sunset, remained as a demonstration of the getting through soul of networks limited by the strings of predetermination. What's more, as sunset hung the town in a sweeping of stars, Eldoria's immortal appeal murmured stories of an excursion that waited in the hearts of the people who called it home.

3.1 The protagonist arrives in Majestic Heights, drawn by a mysterious calling or a personal quest.

In the core of a huge and great scene, settled between transcending tops and encompassed by an ocean of mists, lay Magnificent Levels — a domain covered in secret and charm. The air in Magnificent Levels bore a freshness that indicated the rarified climate of a spot immaculate by the ordinary. It was a place that is known for ethereal excellence, where the sun-kissed mountain ridges sparkled like valuable pearls, and the valleys underneath supported mysteries murmured by the breezes that moved throughout the pinnacles.

The hero, their personality hidden in the fogs of vulnerability, showed up in Great Levels with a reason that rose above the common. The call of fate or the reverberation of an individual mission had directed them to this cryptic domain. Grand Levels, known to not many and worshipped by the people who detected its persona, turned into the background for the hero's unfurling venture.

The town at the lower regions of Lofty Levels invited the hero with a mix of interest and veneration. Local people, receptive to the rhythms of the regular ponders that encompassed them, felt an unobtrusive change in the air as the novice crossed the winding ways that prompted the core of their local area. The hero's appearance was not only an opportunity experience; it was an intermingling of infinite powers that blended the actual substance of Superb Levels.

The town seniors, gatekeepers of old insight went down through ages, detected the appearance of a critical second. Their eyes, endured by the progression of time, mirrored a profundity of grasping that outperformed the promptness of daily existence. As the hero wandered further into the town, the elderly folks met in quiet affirmation of the unfurling fate.

Grand Levels, with its cobblestone roads and interesting cabins, radiated an extraordinary appeal that rose above the actual domain. The hero, directed by an inward compass, felt an attractive draw toward the core of the town — where the texture of reality appeared to meet.

In the town square, encompassed by structures that appeared to repeat the magnificence of the mountains, the hero experienced the town diviner. A figure hung in streaming robes, their eyes aglow with old information, met the hero's look with a knowing grin. Maybe the soothsayer had expected the appearance, their presence an essential piece of the astronomical embroidered artwork woven in Magnificent Levels.

"Welcome, searcher of predetermination," the diviner articulated, their voice conveying the heaviness of predictions carved into the very stones that cleared the town square. "Your process has carried you to Superb Levels, a domain where the reverberations of the past and the murmurs representing things to come dance as one."

The hero, recognizing the diviner's words with a grave gesture, felt the reverberation of truth in the air. Magnificent Levels, it appeared, was a material whereupon fates were painted, and the hero had ventured into a magnum opus really taking shape.

The diviner, with an influx of their hand, welcomed the hero to share the story that had carried them to Lofty Levels. The town square, encompassed by spectators whose eyes reflected the hero's interest, turned into a theater where the strings of individual stories interweaved with the excellent story of the domain.

As the hero talked, the air in Great Levels popped with an energy that rose above the commonplace. The diviner, their faculties sensitive to the rhythmic movement of enormous flows, gestured in quiet affirmation of the hero's journey. Magnificent Levels, it appeared, was not just a background; it was a functioning member in the unfurling show.

The town, when a serene shelter, turned into a bustling place as the hero's presence undulated through the local area. Craftsmans made charms imbued with the embodiment of Magnificent Levels, ranchers offered the abundance of prolific valleys, and researchers dug into old texts that held the keys to opening the secrets murmured by the mountain winds.

Grand Levels, with its pinnacles coming to towards the sky, turned into a safe-haven where the hero's journey unfurled against the scenery of sensational scenes. The peaks, washed in shades of dawn and nightfall, saw the hero's rising as they explored the winding ways that prompted domains hidden in fog and secret.

The town seniors, perceiving the advantageous dance between the hero and Magnificent Levels, accepted the jobs of guides and tutors. Together, they unraveled mysterious images scratched into antiquated stones, communed with the spirits that stayed in the high-elevation domains, and explored the difficulties that tried the hero's purpose.

As the hero dove further into the core of Great Levels, they found gateways to domains outside human ability to grasp. Caves concealed in the fissure of the mountains uncovered old wall paintings that portrayed the repeating idea of presence, and clear pools reflected impressions of domains where time streamed like a waterway with no start or end.

Grand Levels, when a background, arose as a person by its own doing — a conscious power that answered the hero's excursion with murmurs conveyed by the mountain winds. The valleys, reverberating with the stir of leaves and the tunes of concealed birds, became observers to a story that rose above the limits of individual journeys.

Amidst the excursion, the hero confronted preliminaries that tried their actual ability as well as how they might interpret the interconnectedness woven into the actual texture of Lofty Levels. The mountain storms, savage and eccentric, reflected the interior whirlwinds that mixed inside the hero's spirit.

The town at the lower regions, limited by the strings of fate, remained as a guide of help. Local people, propelled by the hero's versatility, offered their abilities and astuteness. Great Levels, it appeared, answered the solidarity produced through shared preliminaries, and the hero's mission turned into a journey that resounded with the aggregate heartbeat of the town.

As the hero climbed to the most elevated tops, Superb Levels divulged its most protected mysteries. Sanctuaries roosted on cliffs, their design mixing flawlessly with the regular shapes of the mountains, housed curios that held the way to opening the hero's definitive reason.

The town diviner, having went with the hero on this excursion of disclosure, remained in quiet thought as antiquated predictions spread out like parchments directed by concealed hands. Lofty Levels, it showed up, had picked the hero as a vessel through which the reverberations of the past and the capability representing things to come joined.

In the shadow of a mountain ridge hallowed place, the hero confronted a disclosure that rose above the limits of mortal comprehension. A vast element, a sign of the actual embodiment of Grand Levels, spoke with the hero through a language that reverberated with the heartbeat of the land.

The experience, saw by the town diviner and the hero's sidekicks, turned into a snapshot of fellowship between the individual and the essential powers that represented Lofty Levels. The hero, their motivation explained, embraced the mantle of a watchman endowed with the safeguarding of the domain's harmony.

As the hero plummeted from the mountain ridges, Glorious Levels breathed out a deep breath — a moan that reverberated through the valleys and resounded in the stir of leaves. The town, having played observer to the hero's extraordinary excursion, remained as a demonstration of the harmonious connection between the individual and the climate.

The town older folks, their eyes mirroring the insight of lifetimes, moved toward the hero with a peaceful seriousness. "You have turned into the epitome of Superb Levels," Oryn, the oldest among them, talked. "Your process has interwoven with the fate of this domain, and as you convey its pith inside you, Grand Levels will persevere through the back and forth movement of time."

The hero, presently a gatekeeper of Grand Levels, decided to remain inside the hug of the town at the lower regions. The bond fashioned through preliminaries and disclosures turned into a heritage that rose above ages. Superb Levels, it appeared, had found a watchman whose fate was perpetually laced with the pinnacles and valleys that shaped the actual soul of the domain.

The town, once a waypoint for the hero's mission, changed into a safe house where the reverberations of Lofty Levels resounded in each stone and each murmured breeze. The locals, propelled by the hero's excursion, kept on living as one with the normal ponders that encompassed them, perceiving their job as stewards of a domain that rose above the standard.

As time unfurled, Glorious Levels and the hero became indistinguishable — an adventure woven into the actual texture of the land. The cobblestone roads, when trampled by the hero as a searcher of fate, reverberated with the giggling of kids and the murmur of day to day existence. Great Levels, it showed up, had found a watchman whose presence reverberated through the ages, a gatekeeper whose story waited in the breezes that murmured through the pinnacles and valleys.

The hero, having satisfied their fate, remained on the town the starting point last time, looking towards the peaks that supported the insider facts and disclosures of Grand Levels. The town diviner, their eyes mirroring the profundity of figuring out that rose above human understanding, moved toward the hero with a knowing grin.

"Your process has turned into a piece of the timeless dance of Glorious Levels," the soothsayer talked. "As the mountains persevere, so will your heritage reverberation through the ages — a demonstration of the interconnectedness of individual fates and the immortal hug of domains outside human ability to comprehend."

3.2 Describe their initial impressions and interactions with the locals.

The hero's appearance in the little waterfront town of Cresthaven denoted the start of an extraordinary excursion. The town, settled between rough precipices and the delicate hug of the sea, oozed an immortal appeal that appeared to repeat the back and forth movement of the tides. The air conveyed an inconspicuous touch of salt, and the far off cries of seagulls highlighted the sea character of Cresthaven.

As the hero ventured onto the endured cobblestone roads, local people cast quick looks toward them. Cresthaven, however familiar with the comings and goings of sailors, only occasionally seen a more interesting whose presence conveyed a demeanor of secret. The townsfolk, their appearances scratched with the accounts of innumerable tides, traded quieted discussions as the hero wandered through the limited rear entryways.

The town square, flanked by interesting shops and clamoring with the exercises of day to day existence, turned into a point of convergence for the hero's underlying cooperations. The smell of newly gotten fish floated from the close by market slows down, blending with the briny aroma of the ocean. Cresthaven's occupants, with endured hands and faces carved by the progression of time, stopped in their day to day schedules to notice the newbie.

The hero, receptive to the subtleties of their environmental factors, moved toward a neighborhood angler who was patching his nets close to the harbor. The angler, squinting against the daylight moving on the water, gazed upward as the hero moved close. A climate beaten cap concealed his eyes, however an inquisitive shine shone underneath the edge.

"Good tidings, stranger," the angler presented with a gesture, his hands deftly working the complexities of the net. "You're far from the standard ports. What carries you to Cresthaven?"

The hero, their eyes mirroring a mix of assurance and interest, discussed an excursion that had driven them to the waterfront town. The angler, however at first held, wound up attracted to the truthfulness the hero's words. The stories of far off lands and unfamiliar oceans ignited a flash of shared experience, and a fellowship started to unfurl underneath the pungent breeze.

As expression of the novice spread through Cresthaven, the hero's presence turned into a subject of vivified conversations in the neighborhood bar. The foundation, with its old wooden inside and the delicate lilt of ocean shanties in the air, filled in as a social occasion place for the townsfolk. The hero, inquisitive to become familiar with Cresthaven and its occupants, wandered into the exuberant foundation.

Local people, situated at worn tables and trading exchange over mugs of brew, looked toward the hero with a blend of interest and neighborliness. A carefully prepared mariner, conspicuous by the ocean endured tattoos that embellished his lower arms, coaxed the novice to join the common table. The bar, it appeared, embraced a custom of shared stories and a feeling of brotherhood that rose above the limits of commonality.

"Come, stranger! Sit, share a story or two," the mariner shouted, his eyes glimmering with the glow of fellowship. "Cresthaven's dependably eager for new stories, particularly from those who've tasted the salt of far off waters."

The hero, their underlying reservations liquefying in the glow of the bar's cordiality, started to share scraps of their excursion. Stories of unfamiliar islands, legendary ocean animals, and the appeal of unseen skylines unfurled like the pages of an awe-inspiring marine adventure. Local people, their consideration enthralled by the hero's words, tracked down an ongoing idea that associated the seaside town to the huge territory of the sea.

In the days that followed, the hero's collaborations with local people became woven into the texture of Cresthaven's day to day routine. The town, at first monitored in its gathering of the outsider, steadily embraced the novice as one of its own. The dough puncher, known for the flavorful fragrance of newly prepared bread that drifted from the shop, offered a portion to the hero as a token of generosity. The old lady who kept an eye on a little nursery close to the town square shared the mysteries of developing solid waterfront blossoms that flourished in the pungent air.

Cresthaven, it appeared, unfurled its layers to the hero as time passes. The townsfolk, with their special eccentricities and shared feeling of local area, turned into a basic piece of the hero's excursion. The youngsters, their giggling reverberating through the rear entryways, respected the outsider with wide-looked at interest, while the seniors, with a gesture and a grin, recognized the ephemerality of life's transient minutes.

The hero, thus, responded the glow of Cresthaven's hug. They helped the nearby angler with the complexities of net repairing, traded stories of far off lands with the mariners who moored in the harbor, and, surprisingly, joined the off the cuff ocean shanties that resonated in the bar's comfortable inside. The bonds produced in the beat of Cresthaven's everyday existence rose above the bounds of language, turning into a quiet grasping that unified the hero with the town's pulse.

At some point, as the sun plunged beneath the skyline, painting the sky in tints of orange and pink, the hero ended up on the bluffs sitting above the tremendous region of the sea. The sound of waves running into the stones underneath conveyed a musical rhythm that reflected the ages old discourse among land and ocean. Cresthaven, with its unassuming roofs and clamoring harbor, appeared as though a shelter supported between the old precipices and the everlasting tides.

As the hero remained on the precipices, a recognizable face drew nearer. It was the angler who had first invited the rookie to Cresthaven. His climate beaten cap currently refreshed in his grasp, and the lines carved all over recounted accounts that could only be described as epic enjoyed pair with the ocean.

"You've become one of us, stranger," the angler commented, his eyes looking at the skyline with a knowing glimmer. "Cresthaven has an approach to meshing strings into the hearts of those wait on its shores. What brings you here isn't simply the call of far off lands, yet the reverberation of an association that rises above the immeasurability of the sea."

The hero, contacted by the angler's words, gestured in quiet affirmation. Cresthaven, it appeared, had become more than a waypoint in their excursion. The town and its occupants had become strings in the embroidery of the hero's story — a story that unfurled together as one of the waterfront breeze and the repeating waves.

The townsfolk, perceiving the cooperative relationship that had bloomed between the hero and Cresthaven, assembled in the town square for a mutual festival. A huge fire popped, projecting a warm gleam that moved according to local people. Fish from the clamoring market sizzled on shoddy barbecues, and the air was loaded up with the melodic types of ocean shanties sung by the accumulated voices.

The hero, remaining in the midst of the party, felt a significant feeling of having a place. Cresthaven, with its immortal appeal and the fellowship of its occupants, had turned into a home amidst the hero's roaming venture. The security manufactured in shared stories, chuckling, and the mood of day to day existence turned into a demonstration of the extraordinary force of local area.

As the festival unfurled, the hero understood that their underlying feelings of Cresthaven had risen above the surface appeal of the beach front town. What had started as a secretive appearance had developed into a harmonious relationship — a common trade that enhanced both the hero and the townsfolk. Cresthaven, it appeared, was not simply a scenery to the hero's excursion but rather a no nonsense person that had turned into a vital piece of their story.

Yet again in the calm minutes that followed the festival, the hero remained on the precipices sitting above the sea. The moon cast a silver sheen on the undulating waves, and the pungent breeze conveyed murmurs of appreciation and kinship. Cresthaven, with its gleaming harbor lights and the far off calls of nighttime seabirds, supported the hero in a quiet hug — a demonstration of the getting through associations woven in the recurring pattern of life.

The following morning, as the hero arranged to proceed with their excursion, the townsfolk accumulated close to the harbor to say goodbye. The angler, his hands currently consistent and endured, caught the hero's shoulder in a token of quiet fellowship. The pastry specialist offered a bag of newly heated products for the street, and the kids, with wide-peered toward interest, introduced little tokens created from shells.

Cresthaven, however said goodbye to the baffling outsider, conveyed the reverberations of their common minutes in the stir of leaves and the delicate lapping of waves. The hero, strolling down the natural cobblestone roads one last time, felt a blend of appreciation and sentimentality for the waterfront town that had turned into a startling sanctuary.

As the hero's outline blurred into the distance, Cresthaven remained as a demonstration of the extraordinary force of chance experiences and the significant associations that could be produced in the most unpretentious of spots. The beach front town, with its immortal appeal and the versatility of its occupants, kept on moving to the mood of the tides — a residing story that unfurled with every dawn and dusk, everlastingly carved in the hearts of the people who called it home.

3.3 Establish the protagonist's goals and motivations for being in Majestic Heights.

The hero's excursion to Lofty Levels was established in an embroidery of objectives and inspirations that unfurled like the stupendous story of a legendary journey. From the second they set foot in the domain, the air humming with the commitment of secret and predetermination, it became obvious that the hero's presence was not erratic; it was directed by a reason that rose above the limits of common presence.

Magnificent Levels, with its transcending tops and perplexing scenes, held privileged insights murmured by the mountain winds and carved into the very stones that cleared the town square. The hero, drawn by an internal compass that reverberated with the grandiose flows of the domain, looked for replies to questions that waited in the openings of their spirit.

As the hero wandered further into Glorious Levels, their objectives started to solidify in the midst of the secrets that unfurled. The old predictions, known to the town elderly folks and scratched into the stones of the hallowed forest, discussed a grandiose combination — a second when predetermination would interlace with the destiny of the actual domain.

The hero's most memorable objective was to disentangle the riddle encompassing their own reality. Murmurs of a heredity laced with the grandiose powers that represented Lofty Levels had arrived at their ears, and a longing for self-disclosure turned into the main impetus behind their excursion. The hero accepted that the responses to their personality lay secret in the old legend watched by the town elderly folks and the magical energies that saturated the high-height domains.

Going with this individual mission was the all-encompassing objective of safeguarding the fragile equilibrium of Superb Levels. The domain, with ethereal magnificence and the dance of sorcery wove through its scenes, confronted an approaching danger. Dim powers, drawn by the hero's excursion and the vast energies that encompassed them, looked to upset the amicable harmony that had supported Magnificent Levels for ages.

The town older folks, caretakers of old insight, perceived the hero as a vital figure in the enormous show that unfurled. Their objective, lined up with the actual substance of Magnificent Levels, was to direct and engage the hero to stand up to the infringing shadows. Together, they left on an aggregate undertaking to interpret secretive engravings, cooperative with magical creatures, and explore the secret corners of the domain where the harmony among light and obscurity wavered on a fragile incline.

The hero's inspirations stretched out past private revelation and the conservation of Great Levels. They held onto a significant feeling of obligation — a comprehension that their process was unpredictably woven into the predeterminations of the locals who called the domain home.

The cooperative connection between the individual and the aggregate turned into a core value, and the hero looked to enable the residents, granting the information and strength expected to endure the preliminaries that lay ahead.

A more profound layer of the hero's inspirations arose as they communed with the enormous substance on the peak place of worship. The disclosure that Glorious Levels itself had a consciousness — a living embodiment that answered the recurring pattern of infinite energies — developed the's comprehension hero might interpret their job. Their objective extended to turn into a stewardship of the domain, a promise to guaranteeing that Lofty Levels persevered as a reference point of wizardry and marvel for a long time into the future.

The hero's excursion, energized by a combination of individual journey and aggregate liability, wandered through the thick woodlands, old destroys, and secret domains that Magnificent Levels revealed. Each step was a hit the dance floor with fate, a complex movement that repeated the enormous flows that pervaded the actual texture of the domain. As they dug into the core of the secret, the hero's inspirations developed, and the objectives that at first appeared to be individualistic converged with the bigger story of Magnificent Levels.

The consecrated woods, washed in the ethereal shine of evening glow, turned into a nexus where the hero got dreams that offered looks into the past and future. The grandiose substance, a sign of the domain's quintessence, spoke with the hero in a language that rose above words. The objectives and inspirations, when covered in vulnerability, tracked down clearness in the fellowship between the individual and the extraordinary powers that administered Glorious Levels.

The hero's relationship with the town senior, Oryn, extended as they uncovered layers of old predictions that predicted an intermingling of fates. Oryn, with the heaviness of gathered shrewdness in his look, turned into a coach and guide, directing the hero through the maze of disclosures and difficulties that Superb Levels introduced. Together, they looked to interpret the enigmatic images carved into the stones and explore the inconspicuous flows of wizardry that beat underneath the outer layer of the domain.

The hero's objectives became interlaced with the actual soul of Glorious Levels. They tried to saddle the inactive capacities of the locals, engaging them to become gatekeepers of their own fate. Craftsmans made apparatuses imbued with the pith of the domain, ranchers took advantage of the ripe energies that moved through the valleys, and researchers uncovered failed to remember texts that held the keys to opening the secrets that lay on pause.

As the hero confronted preliminaries that tried their purpose, Lofty Levels reflected the difficulties in the physical and magical domains.

The thick backwoods, when seen as simple limits, uncovered entrances to domains where time streamed like a waterway with no start or end. The hero's inspirations, established in private disclosure and the safeguarding of the domain, were tried and refined in the cauldron of affliction.

The approaching dimness, an indication of pernicious expectation drawn by the hero's excursion, turned into an imposing enemy. The hero's objectives extended to incorporate the guard of the town and its occupants against the infringing shadows. The once-peaceful safe house changed into a milestone where the conflict among light and murkiness worked out with infinite force.

The hero's inspirations, presently powered by the aggregate strength of the residents and the cooperative bond with Grand Levels, arrived at a pinnacle in the shadow of Eldoria's old wellspring. The climactic showdown with the epitome of haziness turned into a urgent second where individual and aggregate predeterminations combined. The hero, enabled by the solidarity produced through shared preliminaries, vanquished the shadowy foe and reestablished the fragile equilibrium that characterized Glorious Levels.

With the equilibrium reestablished, the hero's objectives went through a transformation. Presently not restricted to the prompt difficulties, their look turned towards the persevering through inheritance they could leave for the domain. The town, having faced the hardship, arose more grounded and more associated than any time in recent memory. The hero, presently a watchman depended with the safeguarding of Great Levels, expected a job that stretched out past the limits of their underlying inspirations.

In the consequence of the grandiose conflict, the hero remained in the town square as an image of versatility and win. Lofty Levels, having seen the hero's excursion, inhaled a deep breath of help. The air snapped with the reverberations of a predetermination satisfied, and the once-covered up objectives of the hero currently remained as support points that upheld the domain's persevering through enchantment.

The hero's inspirations, at first established in private revelation and a feeling of obligation, had become joined with the actual substance of Lofty Levels. The domain, when a scenery, arose as a person that reflected the hero's development and change. The objectives that directed the hero's process turned into a demonstration of the cooperative dance between individual fates and the infinite powers that molded the story of the domain.

As the hero arranged to leave from Magnificent Levels, their objectives had completed the cycle. The puzzler of their own reality, the conservation of the domain, and the strengthening of occupants had combined into a heritage waited in the mountain winds and the stir of leaves.

Magnificent Levels, perpetually different by the hero's appearance, remained as a demonstration of the groundbreaking force of direction and the getting through reverberation of an excursion that rose above the limits of time.

The town senior, Oryn, moved toward the hero with a knowing grin. "Your process has everlastingly changed the woven artwork of Grand Levels," he talked, his eyes mirroring the heaviness of the excursion they had shared. "However, as the flows of fate recurring pattern, the town will persevere, a guide for the individuals who look for shelter and reason."

The hero, their association with Magnificent Levels carved in the chronicles of time, bid goodbye to the domain that had turned into a safe-haven and a pot. As they navigated the cobbled roads one last time, the reverberations of Great Levels' immortal appeal murmured stories of an excursion that waited in the hearts of the people who called it home.

Grand Levels, having endured the hardship and embraced the rhythmic movement of time, remained as a living demonstration of the groundbreaking force of objectives and inspirations that rose above the individual and embraced the aggregate heartbeat of a domain molded by predetermination and wizardry.

The hero's presence in the enchanted domain of Glorious Levels bore the heaviness of significant inspirations, each string of direction entwined into the texture of their excursion. From the exact instant they set foot on the cobblestone roads, the air imbued with the supernatural energy of the transcending tops, it was apparent that the hero's visit rose above simple chance. Lofty Levels, with its ethereal excellence and enormous reverberation, turned into the pot where the hero's inspirations unfurled like petals in a vast blossom.

At the center of the hero's inspirations lay a journey for self-disclosure — an investigation of the mysterious embroidery that included their personality. Murmurs of old predictions, scratched into the stones of the town square and protected by the town seniors, indicated an association between the hero and the actual substance of Lofty Levels. This journey for self-information turned into the compass directing their means through the holy woods and the high-height domains where the murmurs of predetermination waited in the mountain winds.

The hero, with a longing to disentangle the secrets covering their own reality, looked for fellowship with the town older folks. Oryn, the respected pioneer, became both guide and prophet, offering enigmatic experiences into the hero's genealogy and the infinite powers that interweaved with their destiny. The objective of self-revelation, an individual odyssey established in the enormous flows that flooded through Superb Levels, drove the hero to navigate stowed away ways and uncover the mysteries concealed inside the domain's old legend.

As the hero's process unfurled, their inspirations extended to include the protection of Glorious Levels itself. The domain, washed in the gleam of old enchantment, confronted an approaching danger — an obscurity drawn by the hero's excursion and the vast energies that beat inside them. The objective of protecting the fragile equilibrium of Glorious Levels turned into an obligation entwined with the hero's developing comprehension of their part in the enormous story.

The town older folks, perceiving the hero as a key part in the unfurling show, shared dreams of an approaching shadow that tried to overshadow the domain's agreeable balance. The hero's inspirations, presently weaved with the aggregate destiny of Glorious Levels, impelled them into a cooperative undertaking with the elderly folks to translate enigmatic engravings, community with mysterious creatures, and explore the secret corners of the domain where the harmony among light and obscurity wavered on a sensitive incline.

Aggregate liability turned into a characterizing feature of the hero's inspirations. The acknowledgment that their process was not only a singular journey but rather an inestimable union that resounded with the fates of the residents added a layer of intricacy to their objectives. The hero, perceiving the advantageous connection between the individual and the aggregate, looked to enable the residents with the information and strength expected to endure the preliminaries that lay ahead.

Great Levels, with its transcending tops and consecrated forests, unfurled as a living substance — a domain receptive to the rhythmic movement of infinite energies. The hero's inspirations extended to embrace stewardship, a pledge to guaranteeing that Superb Levels persevered as a safe-haven of enchantment and marvel for a long time into the future. The objectives that had at first centered around private disclosure currently converged with a bigger story, repeating the interconnectedness between the individual and the infinite powers that molded the predetermination of the domain.

The holy woods, washed in the ethereal sparkle of evening glow, turned into a nexus where the hero got dreams that offered looks into the past and future. The enormous element on the mountain ridge sanctum spoke with the hero in a language that rose above words, developing comprehension they might interpret the complicated connection between Glorious Levels and their own excursion. The inspirations, when covered in vulnerability, tracked down lucidity in the fellowship between the individual and the supernatural powers that administered the domain.

The hero's relationship with Oryn, the town senior, developed as they uncovered layers of old predictions that anticipated an intermingling of predeterminations. Oryn, with the heaviness of gathered shrewdness in his look, turned into a coach and guide, controlling the hero through the maze of disclosures and difficulties that Grand Levels introduced. Together, they tried to translate the enigmatic images scratched into the stones and explore the inconspicuous flows of wizardry that beat underneath the outer layer of the domain.

Enabling the townspeople turned into a critical part of the hero's inspirations. They tried to tackle the dormant capacities of the local area, changing Superb Levels into a sanctuary where craftsmans made devices imbued with the embodiment of the domain, ranchers took advantage of the prolific energies that moved through the valleys, and researchers uncovered failed to remember texts that held the keys to opening the secrets that lay on pause. The hero's objectives, presently weaved with the aggregate strength of the residents, unfurled as a cooperative work to sustain the domain against the infringing shadows.

Preliminaries that tried the hero's purpose likewise tried the solidarity of the town. The approaching dimness, an indication of pernicious expectation drawn by the hero's excursion, turned into an impressive foe. The hero's inspirations extended to incorporate the protection of the town and its occupants against the infringing shadows. The once-quiet safe house changed into a landmark where the conflict among light and haziness worked out with enormous power.

The hero's inspirations, presently powered by the aggregate strength of the townspeople and the harmonious bond with Glorious Levels, arrived at a peak in the shadow of Eldoria's old wellspring. The climactic showdown with the epitome of obscurity turned into a urgent second where individual and aggregate fates merged. The hero, engaged by the solidarity produced through shared preliminaries, vanquished the shadowy enemy and reestablished the fragile equilibrium that characterized Glorious Levels.

With the equilibrium reestablished, the hero's objectives went through a transformation. As of now not bound to the quick difficulties, their look turned towards the persevering through inheritance they could leave for the domain. The town, having faced the hardship, arose more grounded and more associated than any time in recent memory. The hero, presently a watchman depended with the protection of Superb Levels, expected a job that stretched out past the limits of their underlying inspirations.

In the consequence of the grandiose conflict, the hero remained in the town square as an image of versatility and win. Superb Levels, having seen the hero's excursion, inhaled a deep breath of help. The air popped with the reverberations of a fate satisfied, and the once-covered up objectives of the hero presently remained as support points that upheld the domain's getting through sorcery.

The hero's inspirations, at first established in private disclosure and a feeling of obligation, had become joined with the actual embodiment of Superb Levels. The domain, when a scenery, arose as a person that reflected the hero's development and change. The objectives that directed the hero's process turned into a demonstration of the cooperative dance between individual predeterminations and the enormous powers that formed the story of the domain.

As the hero arranged to leave from Lofty Levels, their objectives had ended up back at square one. The puzzle of their own reality, the protection of the domain, and the strengthening of occupants had joined into a heritage waited in the mountain winds and the stir of leaves. Grand Levels, everlastingly different by the hero's appearance, remained as a demonstration of the extraordinary force of direction and the persevering through reverberation of an excursion that rose above the limits of time.

The town senior, Oryn, moved toward the hero with a knowing grin. "Your process has always modified the woven artwork of Great Levels," he talked, his eyes mirroring the heaviness of the excursion they had shared. "In any case, as the flows of fate recurring pattern, the town will persevere, a reference point for the people who look for shelter and reason."

The hero, their association with Grand Levels carved in the records of time, bid goodbye to the domain that had turned into a safe-haven and a cauldron. As they crossed the cobbled roads one last time, the reverberations of Grand Levels' immortal appeal murmured stories of an excursion that waited in the hearts of the people who called it home.

Glorious Levels, having faced the hardship and embraced the back and forth movement of time, remained as a living demonstration of the groundbreaking force of objectives and inspirations that rose above the individual and embraced the aggregate heartbeat of a domain molded by predetermination and enchantment.

Chapter 4

Unveiling the Hidden Treasures

In the tranquil hallways of time, where the reverberations of the past resound with the present, there lies an embroidery woven with the strings of history, secret, and untold stories. A story traverses the ages, crossing the scenes of failed to remember civic establishments, lost realms, and confounding societies. As we set out on an excursion to disclose the secret fortunes hid inside the folds of time, we strip back the layers of lack of clarity to uncover the extravagance that lies underneath.

The puzzle of stowed away fortunes has dazzled the human creative mind for quite a long time. Whether covered profound inside the earth, hid in antiquated compositions, or protected by the ways of the world, these fortunes allure to the inquisitive, the gutsy, and the valiant spirits who try to uncover the mysteries they hold. The appeal of the obscure, the excitement of disclosure, and the commitment of inconceivable abundance have powered the journeys of voyagers, archeologists, and fortune trackers since the beginning of time.

One of the most unbelievable stories of stowed away fortunes traces all the way back to the time of the Knights Knight, a middle age request covered in secret and interest. The Knights, committed to safeguard travelers on their excursion to the Heavenly Land, amassed huge riches and influence during their prime. Be that as it may, as murmurs of apostasy and trick encompassed them, the request confronted mistreatment, prompting the concealment of the Knights by Lord Philip IV of France in the mid fourteenth hundred years.

Rumors have spread far and wide suggesting that the Knights, expecting their downfall, disguised their fortunes in different areas, shielding their abundance from meddlesome eyes. The whereabouts of these secret reserves have turned into the stuff of legend, rousing incalculable fortune trackers and scheme scholars to leave on missions to uncover the mythical Knight treasures. From the rough scenes of the Blessed Land to the profundities of European woodlands, these searchers have investigated every possibility in their quest for the slippery wealth.

However, the Knight treasures are only a drop in the tremendous expanse of disguised ponders that populate the records of history. The old world, with its bunch developments and societies, holds inside its hug a plenty of unlikely treasures ready to be found. From the mythical city of Atlantis, lost underneath the waves, to the fortunes of the Inca Realm concealed in the core of the Andes, the mysteries of ancient history keep on enticing to the people who set out to unwind the secrets of the past.

In the sands of Egypt, where the pyramids stand as quiet sentinels of a former time, archeologists have uncovered treasures that resist creative mind. The burial chamber of Tutankhamun, found by Howard Carter in 1922, uncovered an abundance of relics, including the well known brilliant cover that decorated the youthful pharaoh's mummy. The fortunes of Tutankhamun offer a brief look into the plushness of old Egyptian civilization, where existence in the wake of death was accepted to be a continuation of natural wonder.

Egypt, nonetheless, isn't the sole overseer of concealed treasures from classical times. In the core of Rome, the city that once governed a realm, lies the Vatican Library, a vault of information and curios that traverses hundreds of years. Inside its consecrated corridors, original copies wrote by the best personalities of the past find asylum, their pages murmuring the mysteries of neglected times. The Vatican Library, with its overly complex files, holds the keys to opening the secrets of history, making it a gold mine for researchers and students of history the same.

As we cross the globe looking for buried treasures, the wildernesses of South America coax with the commitment of antiquated civic establishments and lost urban communities. The Amazon rainforest, with its impervious overhang and thick vegetation, disguises mysteries that have escaped disclosure for a really long time.

Archeologists have uncovered proof of cutting edge social orders, like the strange city of El Dorado, said to be enhanced with gold and untold wealth. The mission for El Dorado has driven voyagers to the profundities of the Amazon, where the lavish plant life conceals the remainders of a development that once flourished in segregation.

In Asia, the Silk Street remains as a demonstration of the interconnectedness of societies and the trading of merchandise and thoughts. Along this antiquated shipping lane, dealers and voyagers exchanged products as well as stories of stowed away fortunes and intriguing terrains. The legendary city of Shangri-La, settled in the Himalayas, catches the creative mind with its idealistic appeal. Supposed to be a safe-haven of harmony and illumination, Shangri-La stays a puzzler, enticing explorers to leave on unsafe excursions looking for this legendary heaven.

The journey for buried treasures isn't restricted to the domains of history and legend; it stretches out into the domain of craftsmanship and inventiveness. The workmanship world, with its show-stoppers and unseen jewels, holds prizes that rise above the material domain. Lost works by prestigious specialists, taken canvases that have evaporated into the shadows, and neglected models ready to be rediscovered structure an embroidery of creative secrets.

The narrative of stowed away craftsmanship loves frequently entwines with the hazier sections of history, where wars, burglary, and political interest play had an impact in the vanishing of precious works.

The plundering of craftsmanship during The Second Great War, for instance, prompted the disappearing of endless magnum opuses, some of which still can't seem to reemerge. The fastidious endeavors of workmanship analysts and compensation drives look to uncover these buried fortunes and reestablish them to their legitimate spot in the social legacy of mankind.

In the realm of writing, stowed away fortunes appear as failed to remember original copies, lost sonnets, and unseen compositions by scholarly monsters. The Brontë sisters, popular for their books, for example, "Jane Eyre" and "Wuthering Levels," abandoned a stash of unpublished works that have as of late become known. These secret abstract diamonds give new bits of knowledge into the personalities of the Brontës and add to the tradition of their artistic commitments.

The quest for buried treasures reaches out past the physical and creative domains; it dives into the secrets of science and the universe. The universe, with its huge breadth and strange domains, hides mysteries that challenge how we might interpret presence. Dull matter, dark openings, and infinite peculiarities that evade location structure the vast embroidered artwork that researchers attempt to disentangle.

In the mission to uncover the secret fortunes of the universe, stargazers and physicists peer into the profundities of room, utilizing telescopes and instruments that broaden the scope of human discernment. The secrets of the universe, from the starting points of the universe to the idea of extraterrestrial life, stay tricky, welcoming the curious personalities of researchers to push the limits of information.

Nearer to home, the profundities of the seas harbor stowed away fortunes that rival the secrets of space. Underneath the waves, where daylight battles to enter, lie neglected domains overflowing with life and unseen miracles. Lowered urban communities, lost developments, and marine living things yet to be ordered structure the lowered woven artwork of the maritime profundities.

The submerged city of Atlantis, a fantasy that has enthralled the creative mind for quite a long time, represents the charm of stowed away fortunes underneath the waves. While the presence of Atlantis stays an issue of discussion among researchers, the seas have uncovered old wrecks, lost developments, and lowered scenes that revise the story of mankind's set of experiences. Submerged prehistoric studies, with its specific methods and innovations, opens a window into the past that was recently clouded by the waters' hug.

The quest for buried treasures isn't without its difficulties and hazards. The journey for riches, information, and revelation frequently includes some major disadvantages, testing the restrictions of human versatility and assurance. Stories of lost campaigns, unsafe excursions, and the penances made for the sake of uncovering the obscure add a layer of intricacy to the story of stowed away fortunes.

In the wildernesses of Focal America, the narrative of Hiram Bingham and the revelation of Machu Picchu epitomizes the difficulties looked by those in quest for buried ponders. Bingham, an American pilgrim, coincidentally found the old Inca fortress in 1911, concealed in the midst of the Andean pinnacles. The strenuous excursion, loaded with impediments and risks, finished in the disclosure of one of the best archeological finds of the twentieth hundred years.

Essentially, the quest for the Northwest Section, a legendary ocean course through the Icy, drove wayfarers to defy cruel environments, slippery ice floes, and the consistently present phantom of detachment and passing. The journey for buried courses and strange domains pushed the limits of human investigation yet additionally demanded a cost for the people who considered wandering into the frosty unexplored world.

In the domain of stowed away fortunes, the quest for information frequently entwines with the hunger for influence and control. The stealthy universe of surveillance, with its clandestine tasks and grouped data, is a theater where secret fortunes appear as state insider facts, knowledge records, and characterized innovations.

The Virus War time, set apart by philosophical struggles and international strains, saw the rise of spies and knowledge organizations took part in a worldwide mental contest.

The narratives of Cold Conflict reconnaissance, from the Cambridge Spy Ring to the Cuban Rocket Emergency, uncover the many-sided dance among mystery and disclosure. The secret fortunes of undercover work, whether as arranged reports or encoded messages, hold the keys to figuring out the clandestine battles that formed the course of history. Many years after the fact, declassified records and disclosures shed light on the shadowy universe of reconnaissance, offering a brief look into the secret components of worldwide governmental issues.

In the time of innovation, the computerized domain turns into a milestone for buried fortunes and network safety. The immense organizations of the internet, with their complex codes and scrambled information, hide treasures as delicate data, monetary records, and protected innovation. The ascent of cybercrime and digital fighting presents another boondocks where secret fortunes are not covered in the earth but rather concealed inside the huge territory of the computerized scene.

The journey for buried treasures, whether in the physical or advanced domain, frequently prompts moral predicaments and moral scrapes. The allotment of social antiquities, the double-dealing of normal assets, and the outcomes of unrestrained investigation bring up issues about the obligations that accompany the quest for information and abundance. The fortunes of the earth, whether concealed in the profundities of the sea or covered underneath layers of soil, convey with them a heritage that rises above the limits of time.

As we consider the embroidery of stowed away fortunes woven through the ages, we come to understand that the journey for the obscure is a major part of the human experience. From the old developments that looked to deify their accomplishments in secret burial chambers to the cutting edge voyagers who test the universe for grandiose mysteries, the craving to uncover stowed away ponders is a string that ties us across reality.

The revealing of stowed away fortunes isn't only an actual undertaking; it is an excursion of the psyche and soul. The fortunes we look for may not generally be substantial; they might appear as information, shrewdness, and the comprehension of our position in the amazing embroidery of presence. The quest for buried treasures, whether in the domains of history, workmanship, science, or the universe, is a demonstration of the human limit with respect to interest, investigation, and the steady journey for revelation.

Eventually, the secret fortunes we reveal are not just ancient rarities or wealth; they are windows into the tremendous scene of human potential and the boundless conceivable outcomes that anticipate the people who set out to wander into the unexplored world.

As we stand on the edge representing things to come, the secret fortunes that lie before us coax with the commitment of new skylines, untold revelations, and the continuation of an excursion that rises above the limits of time and creative mind.

4.1 The protagonist begins to uncover the secrets hidden within Majestic Heights.

In the core of the beautiful town of Great Levels, where ivy-clad chateaus and cobblestone roads make a climate of immortal polish, the hero sets out on an excursion that will unwind the mysteries hid inside the town's puzzling exterior. Lofty Levels, with its noteworthy appeal and cultured façade, holds more going on than might be expected. Past the cleaned outside of its impressive homes and manicured gardens, a maze of secrets anticipates, covered in murmurs and monitored by the shadows of the past.

The hero, an inquisitive and perceptive soul, at first shows up in Glorious Levels without any notion of the mysteries that lie underneath the surface. Drawn by the town's ideal appeal and the commitment of a new beginning, they become an occupant in one of the Victorian-time houses that line the roads like quiet sentinels of a former period. Much to their dismay that their appearance will get under way a chain of occasions that will strip back the layers of Great Levels' set of experiences, uncovering an embroidery woven with interest, embarrassment, and long-covered mysteries.

As the hero sinks into their new habitation, a feeling of disquiet creeps in, similar to the main unpretentious notes of a frightful song. Lofty Levels, with its very much manicured yards and all around saved engineering, harbors a quiet pressure that waits all around. The townsfolk, respectful and welcoming on a superficial level, trade monitored looks and talk in quieted tones when the hero cruises by. It becomes clear that underneath the facade of people who value proper etiquette, Great Levels harbors an aggregate quiet — a common mystery that ties the local area in a settlement of circumspection.

The hero's excursion of disclosure starts guiltlessly enough — an old photo concealed in the storage room, a blurred letter tracked down in a dusty corner of the library. These apparently unimportant relics become the breadcrumbs that lead the hero down a deep, dark hole of interest. The photo, showing a get-together of townsfolk in clothing from a former period, holds faces frozen in time, their looks alluding to untold stories and secret feelings.

The blurred letter, written in exquisite content, discusses illegal love, surreptitious gatherings, and the lengths to which some would go to protect the sacredness of cultural assumptions. As the hero dives further into the town's chronicles, pouring over neglected reports and diaries, a story unfurls — a story of adoration and misfortune, of desires squashed underneath the heaviness of custom, and of a local area limited by privileged insights that won't be covered.

Superb Levels, it turns out to be clear, was not generally the peaceful sanctuary it seems, by all accounts, to be. In the late nineteenth hundred years, the town took the stand concerning a progression of outrages that shook its establishments. Relationships that challenged cultural standards, business competitions that turned destructive, and a misfortune that made a permanent imprint on the shared perspective of the town — this multitude of components mix into a perplexing snare of privileged insights that have been painstakingly protected through ages.

The hero's mission for truth takes them to the core of Magnificent Levels — the town square, where an old oak tree remains as a quiet observer to the progression of time. Neighborhood old stories talks about the tree's importance, connecting it to the town's establishing and the occasions that molded its predetermination. Underneath its branches, the hero finds a secret niche, a little depression in the storage compartment that holds a reserve of letters, journals, and curios that act as a period case of Superb Levels' turbulent past.

As the hero filters through the items in the secret recess, a story arises — a story of prohibited love between two conspicuous families, a business contention that swelled into misfortune, and the resulting conceal that fashioned the town's veneer of decency. The hero turns into an incidental criminal investigator, sorting out the riddle of Grand Levels' set of experiences, directed by the vaporous murmurs of the past.

The town's occupants, at first careful about the hero's requests, step by step open up as trust is procured. Older folks share stories went down through ages, winding around an embroidery of recollections that rises above time. Every disclosure adds a layer to the town's mind boggling story, uncovering the human show that unfurled in secret and the outcomes that formed Magnificent Levels' present.

As the hero reveals the mysteries concealed inside Magnificent Levels, they end up entrapped in a trap of feelings — compassion for the characters of the past, outrage at the treacheries executed, and a feeling of obligation to uncover reality. The once-peaceful roads of Grand Levels become the stage for an excursion of recovery and compromise, as the hero tries to accommodate the wrongdoings of the past with the present-day repercussions that wait like phantoms in the shared mindset of the town.

The hero's process becomes interwoven with the existences of the relatives of the individuals who formed Grand Levels' set of experiences. Family treasures, long-neglected photos, and oral practices went down through ages give looks into the individual battles and wins of the people who explored the turbulent waters of adoration, desire, and cultural assumptions.

In their quest for truth, the hero finds that uncovering the mysteries of Lofty Levels requires more than verifiable exploration — it requests a comprehension of the complexities of human connections, the delicacy of notoriety, and the lengths to which people will go to safeguard their heritages. The once-lifeless engineering of the town takes on an unmistakable overflow of energy, turning into a quiet observer to the hero's mission for equity and compromise.

The hero's endeavors to accommodate the past with the current face opposition from certain quarters of Great Levels. The town's gentry, gripping to the remainders of their progenitors' heritage, view the hero's requests as a danger to the painstakingly developed story that safeguards their standing. Strains ascend as the hero rocks the boat, uncovering covered bits of insight that shake the groundworks of the town's laid out pecking order.

In the midst of the strife, the hero finds a far-fetched partner as a nearby history specialist, a whimsical figure with a propensity for unwinding the secrets of Magnificent Levels. Together, they dig further into the town's chronicles, uncovering failed to remember antiques and neglected subtleties that give new viewpoints on the occasions that formed Great Levels' predetermination.

The story goes off in strange directions as the hero's excursion of disclosure turns into an impetus for change inside Great Levels. The disclosures, once restricted to the shadows, spill out of the dark, compelling the townsfolk to face the awkward bits of insight that have formed their lives. Injuries from way back are returned, yet all the while, the local area starts to mend, and the phantoms of the past track down a similarity to goal.

The hero's journey for truth, when a single undertaking, develops into a collective investigation of personality, pardoning, and the common obligation of protecting the town's inheritance. Great Levels, when a stronghold of quietness and privileged insights, turns into a material whereupon the inhabitants paint another story — one that recognizes the imperfections of the past while embracing the potential for development and recovery.

In the last sections of the hero's excursion, the mysteries concealed inside Superb Levels are revealed. The once-murmured stories become piece of the town's living history, a demonstration of the strength of the human soul and the limit with respect to change. Magnificent Levels, with its ivy-clad manors and cobblestone roads, turns into an image of resurrection, a town that defies its past with fortitude and embraces a future based on the underpinnings of truth and understanding.

As the hero ponders their excursion, they understand that the genuine fortunes of Magnificent Levels are not secret in dusty niches or failed to remember lofts; they are the securities manufactured through shared battles, the compassion developed through understanding, and the strength that arises when a local area defies its devils.

The mysteries might have been divulged, however the hero leaves Superb Levels with a significant feeling of association with its set of experiences and a confident expectation of the sections yet to be written in the town's continuous adventure.

4.2 Explore ancient artifacts, hidden caves, or mystical elements that hold clues to Kilimanjaro's secrets.

Settled in the core of East Africa, the transcending presence of Mount Kilimanjaro orders consideration, its snow-covered tops coming to towards the sky. However, past its lofty outside lies a domain of secrets and untold privileged insights that have enthralled the minds of travelers, globe-trotters, and researchers for a really long time. Kilimanjaro, with its rich woven artwork of land ponders and social importance, covers antiquated ancient rarities, stowed away caverns, and magical components that guarantee to open the privileged insights concealed inside its hug.

At the lower regions of Kilimanjaro, archeological campaigns have uncovered a mother lode of old curios, revealing insight into the locale's profound verifiable roots. The remainders of past civic establishments, covered underneath layers of soil and time, recount an account of human life that originates before the mountain's topographical loftiness. Instruments, earthenware, and leftovers of residences give looks into the existences of the individuals who once called the inclines of Kilimanjaro home, unwinding a story that traverses centuries.

The curios, carefully classified and considered, become entrances to the past, offering experiences into the traditions, convictions, and day to day schedules of antiquated societies that flourished in the shadow of Kilimanjaro. The archeological destinations spread around the mountain, from the fields underneath to the higher heights, structure a riddle ready to be sorted out — a riddle that holds the keys to grasping the cooperative connection among mankind and the stunning presence of Kilimanjaro.

Among the most interesting disclosures are old stone artworks that enhance the caverns and bluffs encompassing Kilimanjaro. The dynamic tones of red, ochre, and white portray scenes of day to day existence, profound ceremonies, and the different natural life that once wandered the locale. These compositions, a demonstration of the creative articulations of old societies, act as a visual file of when Kilimanjaro took the stand concerning the rhythmic movement of human life.

The secret caverns, disguised inside the folds of Kilimanjaro's tough territory, coax pilgrims with the commitment of additional disclosures. Caves, some of which have stayed immaculate for quite a long time, may hold unseen curios, old compositions, or even entombment destinations that develop the secret of Kilimanjaro's past. The underground domain underneath the mountain turns into a material whereupon history is carved as cave rock formations, stalagmites, and the reverberations of ages a distant memory.

The investigation of stowed away caverns requires a fragile harmony among safeguarding and disclosure. Archeologists and spelunkers furnished with current innovation explore the tangled sections, directed by the weak hints of history that wait inside the murkiness. Each step, each painstakingly unearthed layer of residue, divulges a piece of the riddle, enhancing how we might interpret the human excursion in the shadow of Kilimanjaro.

As travelers adventure further into the core of Kilimanjaro, they might experience supernatural components that obscure the lines among the real world and fables. The mountain, worshipped by neighborhood networks as a hallowed element, is interlaced with fantasies and legends that rise above ages. Antiquated stories talk about spirits living inside the mountain's pinnacles, watchmen of its privileged insights and authorities of its secrets.

A few fantasies recount stowed away entryways inside the mountain, doors to different domains that must be gotten to by those considered commendable. These supernatural components, woven into the social texture of the district, add a layer of charm to Kilimanjaro's appeal. Voyagers, roused by the murmurs of neighborhood old stories, may wind up on a journey for substantial relics as well as for the immaterial pith that makes Kilimanjaro a nexus of the mysterious and the commonplace.

Among the supernatural components related with Kilimanjaro is the confidence in recuperating properties ascribed to its glacial masses and mineral-rich waters. Nearby people group, drawing on exceptionally old customs, attribute helpful excellencies to the mountain's assets. The icy masses, accepted to have helpful abilities, are objections for journeys looking for physical and otherworldly recharging. The ethereal association between the regular components of Kilimanjaro and the prosperity of the individuals who occupy its environmental factors adds an element of enchantment to the mountain's heritage.

The quest for Kilimanjaro's privileged insights stretches out past the substantial and enchanted to the domain of natural marvels. The mountain, with its different biological systems going from lavish rainforests to snow capped deserts, harbors a rich biodiversity that has adjusted to the difficulties presented by its transcending presence. Novel plant species, slippery fauna, and transitory examples add to the mind boggling woven artwork of life that flourishes in the shadow of Kilimanjaro.

Researchers and preservationists, drawn by the environmental wonders of Kilimanjaro, participate in examinations that go past the surface to figure out the sensitive equilibrium of its biological systems. Environmental change, deforestation, and the effect of human exercises present dangers to the mountain's normal miracles. The mysteries concealed inside Kilimanjaro's environmental elements become basic snippets of data in the continuous work to safeguard and safeguard this regular fortune.

The investigation of Kilimanjaro's secrets isn't without challenges. The rising to its pinnacles, arriving at heights that test the restrictions of human perseverance, requests actual versatility and mental strength. The unusual weather conditions, the diminishing air, and the consistently present gamble of height related diseases establish a climate where just the most resolved can wander. The quest for Kilimanjaro's insider facts requires a mission for information as well as a showdown with the powers of nature that shape the mountain's personality.

Past the actual difficulties, there is the human part of Kilimanjaro's mysteries — the accounts of the networks that have lived in its shadow for ages. Nearby aides, narrators, and watchmen of oral practices become significant mates on the excursion of investigation. Their experiences, went down through ages, add profundity to the story of Kilimanjaro and make a scaffold between the past and the present.

Over unwinding Kilimanjaro's privileged insights, adventurers might experience the strength of the Chaga public, whose association with the mountain isn't only physical however profound. The Chaga, with their rich social legacy, offer viewpoints on Kilimanjaro that reach out past the logical and archeological. The mountain, to them, isn't simply a geographical development yet a living substance with a spirit that reverberates with the rhythms of life.

The zenith of the investigation excursion might prompt the highest point of Kilimanjaro, where the air is slim, and the all encompassing perspective stretches as may be obvious. The culmination, where earth meets sky, turns into a vantage point from which the privileged insights concealed inside the mountain are uncovered. The physical and allegorical levels arrived at by the adventurer represent the victory of interest, assurance, and the resolute human soul chasing information.

As the adventurer looks at the scene underneath, with Kilimanjaro at their feet, they understand that the privileged insights uncovered are not simple curios or legends. Kilimanjaro's insider facts are a demonstration of the interconnectedness of humankind and the normal world, an update that the quest for information is an excursion that rises above time, borders, and the constraints of our comprehension.

The investigation of old curios, stowed away caverns, and magical components inside the hug of Kilimanjaro turns into a similitude for the general human mission for understanding and association. Kilimanjaro, with its transcending tops and secret miracles, welcomes us to investigate the actual world as well as the profundities of our own interest, flexibility, and the common tradition of mankind on this radiant planet. In the shadow of Kilimanjaro, the mysteries uncovered are not restricted to the actual mountain but rather reverberate with the reverberations of the human soul that sets out on the everlasting excursion of investigation and disclosure.

4.3 Introduce challenges and obstacles that the protagonist must overcome.

In the domain of narrating, the excursion of a hero is frequently set apart by difficulties and impediments that act as pots for character improvement, testing the restrictions of flexibility, assurance, and the natural limit with respect to development. As our story unfurls, our hero ventures into a world loaded with obstacles, both inside and outside, every obstruction a venturing stone on the way of self-revelation and change.

From the actual commencement of our hero's process, the seeds of challenge are planted. It could appear as an inner turmoil — a contention of character, a fight with self-question, or the heaviness of a past that won't be shaken off. The hero's inward scene turns into a milestone where the powers of dread, vulnerability, and the obscure merge. These difficulties, however elusive, are considerable enemies that request thoughtfulness and self-acknowledgment.

Remotely, the world our hero explores is certainly not a generous one. Maybe they end up in an unfriendly climate, where the components contrive against them — a constant desert sun, unforgiving cold breezes, or the thick foliage of an impervious wilderness. Nature, with its imposing magnificence and unyielding power, turns into an impressive foe that tests the hero's endurance senses and versatility.

In the social woven artwork of the hero's reality, challenges assume the appearance of connections stressed by misconception, treachery, or clashing interests. The bonds they structure, whether familial, heartfelt, or dispassionate, become the two wellsprings of solidarity and possible wellsprings of contention. Trust broke, loyalties tried, and partnerships framed or broken — each relational dynamic presents difficulties that shape the hero's direction.

As the hero sets out on their mission, a story unfurls, woven with the strings of difficulties that go past the individual and relational. Maybe they end up caught in the ruses of a strong foe — a main bad guy whose thought processes and activities push the story forward. This outside struggle, whether driven by desire, retribution, or a conflict of philosophies, fills in as a cauldron that tempers the hero's courage.

In the domain of the fantastical, challenges take on a legendary shade. The hero experiences animals of legend — winged serpents that gatekeeper desired treasures, legendary creatures that test the legend's mind and boldness, or old watchmen that stand sentinel over prohibited domains. Each experience with the fantastical stances challenges that rise above the customary, welcoming the hero to stand up to the phenomenal.

The progression of time turns into a partner and an enemy. The ticking clock, whether figurative or unmistakable, presents a transient test — a test of skill and endurance to disentangle a secret, achieve a journey, or forestall a looming disaster.

The criticalness forced by time increases the stakes, driving the hero into a persistent pursuit against the unavoidable walk of seconds, minutes, and hours.

Monetary difficulties may likewise shape the hero's excursion, whether they are confronted with monetary imperatives, financial aberrations, or the battle for endurance notwithstanding financial disparity. The quest for dreams, desires, or the fundamental necessities of life turns into a difficult task, reflecting the financial difficulties that reverberate with this present reality battles numerous people face.

In the maze of the brain, the hero might wrestle with mental difficulties — injuries that torment their past, fears that cripple their present, or the shadow of an obscure future that weavers their mind. Mental and close to home deterrents become scenes to cross, adding layers of intricacy to the hero's inner excursion.

The call to experience, a proclaiming second that entices the hero into the obscure, is in many cases joined by a tutor figure who guides, challenges, and bestows shrewdness. However, this tutor understudy relationship isn't without its preliminaries. The hero might confront the test of tolerating mentorship, confiding in their aide, or accommodating with the unavoidable second when the mentee should outperform the tutor.

Chasing an objective or the disentangling of a secret, the hero might experience riddles, conundrums, and puzzlers that request scholarly ability and critical thinking abilities. The difficulties become cerebral, welcoming the hero — and likewise, the crowd — to participate in a psychological dance that rises above the actual limitations of the story.

As the hero advances on their excursion, the ghost of disappointment turns into an approaching test. Whether driven by outer tensions or inward frailties, the anxiety toward missing the mark, concerning not satisfying hopes, turns into a shadow that canines all their means. Beating the apprehension about disappointment, embracing weakness, and tracking down the boldness to drive forward despite potential loss become vital crossroads in the hero's circular segment.

Some of the time, the test lies as moral situations — decisions that test the hero's ethical compass, driving them to face shades of dark in a world frequently seen clearly. The choices made, the collusions framed, and the penances persevered through become moral difficulties that shape the hero's character and moral fiber.

In the great embroidery of the hero's excursion, the test of progress and change arises as a critical subject. The solace of the natural, the protection from advancing conditions, and the apprehension about venturing into the obscure all add to the test of embracing change. The hero's transformation — from who they were toward the start of the story to who they become by the story's end — is a demonstration of their capacity to explore the flows of change.

Love, as a power both sustaining and turbulent, presents its own arrangement of difficulties. Heartfelt ensnarements, familial bonds, and fellowships become cauldrons that test the hero's ability to cherish, trust, and manufacture associations. The difficulties of adoration might appear as disaster, selling out, or the penance expected for the sake of a more noteworthy reason.

The excursion of the hero is a repetitive one, set apart by repeating difficulties that request development and development. The recurrent nature might appear as rehashing designs, unsettled clashes, or the arrival of past enemies. Every emphasis of the test turns into a chance for the hero to exhibit examples learned, flexibility acquired, and the insight procured on their excursion.

The hero's process is certainly not a singular one; it converges with the existences of different characters, each with their own arrangement of difficulties and snags. The elements of these connections — whether coalitions, clashes, or surprising associations — add to the aggregate difficulties that shape the account. The interconnectedness of difficulties winds around a trap of intricacy that reflects the complexities of the human experience.

Despite challenges, the hero's munitions stockpile incorporates actual strength as well as versatility, mind, compassion, and the limit with regards to self-reflection. The moves become open doors for the hero to take advantage of inactive possibilities, uncover stowed away qualities, and find aspects of their personality that no one but difficulty can uncover.

The goal of difficulties isn't clear 100% of the time. The hero might encounter mishaps, disappointments, and snapshots of hopelessness. The excursion turns into a rollercoaster of wins and hardships, making a story strain that keeps the crowd connected with and put resources into the hero's destiny. The difficulties, a long way from being outlandish barriers, become the impetuses for an extraordinary odyssey.

As the hero defies and vanquishes each test, they arise not as a perfect legend but rather as a nuanced, multi-layered character. The scars of fights battled, the examples gained from disappointments, and the flexibility produced in the cauldron of difficulties shape a hero who is engaging, bona fide, and at last human.

The goal of difficulties isn't the finish of the hero's excursion however a take-off point for new undertakings and unfamiliar domains. The difficulties conquer become the establishment for the following period of the story, welcoming the crowd to go on close by the hero on their steadily developing odyssey.

In the great embroidery of narrating, difficulties and hindrances are not simple story gadgets; they are the twist and weft that make the texture of a convincing, resounding account.

The hero's excursion, interspersed by snapshots of misfortune, win, and thoughtfulness, turns into a mirror mirroring the general human experience — an excursion set apart by difficulties that shape, characterize, and at last enlighten the way toward self-revelation and development.

In the immense material of narrating, the hero's process is frequently woven with a rich embroidery of difficulties and hindrances, making a story dynamic that drives the person toward development, self-revelation, and change. These difficulties, both interior and outside, act as cauldrons that test the restrictions of the hero's flexibility, boldness, and limit with regards to change. As our story unfurls, we set out on an excursion close by the hero, navigating the scenes of misfortune and win that shape their personality.

At the beginning of the hero's excursion, inward difficulties arise as impressive enemies. The thoughtful fight inside their own mind might appear as a contention of personality, a battle against self-question, or the frightful ghost of a past that will not be let go. The hero, exploring the maze of their own contemplations and feelings, faces the test of going up against internal evil presences and defeating the shadows that take steps to darken their way.

Outside challenges, frequently reflecting the cruel real factors of the world, add to the intricacy of the hero's excursion. The actual world turns into a phase where nature itself can be both a partner and a foe. Whether confronting the tenacious components of a cruel climate — a singing desert, frigid tundra, or thick wilderness — or wrestling with the powers of nature, the hero experiences difficulties that request versatility, endurance senses, and an unfaltering determination.

In the unpredictable social embroidery of the hero's reality, challenges assume the appearance of connections stressed by false impressions, treacheries, or clashing interests. The bonds they structure, whether familial, heartfelt, or dispassionate, become the two wellsprings of solidarity and expected wellsprings of contention. Trust broke, loyalties tried, and collusions framed or broken — each relational dynamic presents difficulties that shape the hero's direction and test the flexibility of their associations.

The story bend might acquaint the hero with a strong enemy — a main bad guy whose thought processes and activities impel the story forward. This outside struggle, whether driven by private quarrels, philosophical conflicts, or the quest for power, fills in as a pot that tempers the hero's grit. The difficulties presented by these hostile powers become achievements in the hero's development, requesting key reasoning, boldness, and the manufacturing of collusions to defeat apparently unfavorable chances.

In the fantastical domains of narrating, challenges take on a legendary aspect. The hero experiences animals of legend — winged serpents monitoring desired treasures, legendary creatures testing the legend's mind and mental fortitude, or antiquated gatekeepers standing sentinel over illegal domains.

The difficulties presented by the fantastical components rise above the normal, welcoming the hero to defy the exceptional and explore an existence where reality and legend entwine.

Time, frequently an unrelenting power, presents its own arrangement of difficulties. The ticking clock, whether figurative or unmistakable, forces a fleeting desperation — a looming cutoff time, a test of skill and endurance to unwind a secret, achieve a mission, or forestall an approaching disaster. The test becomes the outside limitations of time as well as the inside tension of living up to assumptions and going up against the certainty of the progression of time.

Monetary difficulties might shape the hero's excursion, acquainting battles related with monetary requirements, financial abberations, or the quest for dreams notwithstanding financial imbalance. The hero wrestles with the difficulties of endurance, yearnings, or exploring the intricacies of an existence where monetary variables play a characterizing job in molding fates.

The hero might stand up to mental difficulties, wrestling with injuries from quite a while ago, fears that cripple their present, or the shadow of an obscure future that weavers their mind. The investigation of mental and close to home deterrents turns into a powerful scene to cross, adding layers of intricacy to the hero's inner excursion.

The call to experience, the proclaiming second that entices the hero into the obscure, frequently accompanies a tutor figure. Nonetheless, the guide understudy relationship isn't without its difficulties. The hero might confront the inside challenge of tolerating mentorship, confiding in their aide, or accommodating with the unavoidable second when the mentee should outperform the guide.

Chasing after objectives or the disentangling of secrets, the hero experiences riddles, conundrums, and mysteries that request scholarly ability and critical thinking abilities. The difficulties become cerebral, welcoming the hero — and likewise, the crowd — to take part in a psychological dance that rises above the actual limitations of the story.

The feeling of dread toward disappointment poses a potential threat as a test. Driven by outer tensions or inward instabilities, the hero wrestles with the apprehension about missing the mark, concerning not satisfying hopes. Conquering the anxiety toward disappointment turns into a pivotal occasion, requiring the hero to embrace weakness, gain from misfortunes, and track down the fortitude to continue on despite expected rout.

Moral issues present difficulties that test the hero's ethical compass. Decisions made, collusions framed, and forfeits persevered through become moral difficulties that shape the hero's character and moral fiber. The choices they face become standards that characterize the moral limits of their personality and set out to arrive at their excursion.

The test of progress and change arises as a vital subject. The solace of the natural, the protection from advancing conditions, and the apprehension about venturing into the obscure add to the test of embracing change. The hero's transformation — from who they were toward the start of the story to who they become by the story's end — is a demonstration of their capacity to explore the flows of change.

Love, both sustaining and wild, presents its own arrangement of difficulties. Heartfelt snares, familial bonds, and companionships become cauldrons that test the hero's ability to cherish, trust, and fashion associations. The difficulties of adoration might appear as grievousness, treachery, or the penances expected for the sake of a more prominent reason.

The progression of time becomes repeating, set apart by repeating difficulties that request development and advancement. Whether confronting rehashing designs, unsettled clashes, or the arrival of past foes, every cycle of the test turns into a chance for the hero to show illustrations learned, versatility acquired, and the insight procured on their excursion.

The hero's process is certainly not a lone one; it converges with the existences of different characters, each with their own arrangement of difficulties and obstructions. The elements of these connections — whether collusions, clashes, or unforeseen associations — add to the aggregate difficulties that shape the story. The interconnectedness of difficulties winds around a snare of intricacy that reflects the complexities of the human experience.

Despite challenges, the hero's munititions stockpile incorporates actual strength as well as versatility, mind, sympathy, and the limit with respect to self-reflection. The provokes become open doors for the hero to take advantage of inactive possibilities, uncover stowed away qualities, and find features of their personality that no one but affliction can uncover.

The goal of difficulties isn't direct all the time. The hero might encounter misfortunes, disappointments, and snapshots of depression. The excursion turns into a rollercoaster of wins and hardships, making story pressure that keeps the crowd connected with and put resources into the hero's destiny. The difficulties, a long way from being outlandish road obstructions, become the impetuses for a groundbreaking odyssey.

As the hero defies and overcomes each test, they arise not as a faultless legend but rather as a nuanced, complex person. The scars of fights battled, the illustrations gained from disappointments, and the versatility produced in the pot of difficulties shape a hero who is engaging, bona fide, and at last human.

The goal of difficulties isn't the finish of the hero's excursion yet a take-off point for new undertakings and strange domains. The difficulties beat become the establishment for the following period of the account, welcoming the crowd to go on close by the hero on their consistently developing odyssey.

In the great embroidery of narrating, difficulties and impediments are not simple story gadgets; they are the twist and weft that make the texture of a convincing, full story. The hero's excursion, interspersed by snapshots of difficulty, win, and thoughtfulness, turns into a mirror mirroring the widespread human experience — an excursion set apart by difficulties that shape, characterize, and at last enlighten the way toward self-disclosure and development.

Chapter 5

Local Wisdom and Guidance

Nearby insight and direction assume a urgent part in molding the social, social, and moral texture of a local area. This supply of aggregate information, went down through ages, is an impression of the special encounters, values, and viewpoints of a specific region. While modernization and globalization have achieved huge changes in different parts of life, nearby insight stays a strong power, giving a feeling of personality and congruity to networks all over the planet.

In numerous social orders, nearby insight is profoundly entwined with the common habitat. Native people group, for example, frequently have a perplexing comprehension of their environments, acquired through hundreds of years of perception and collaboration. This information envelops manageable horticultural practices, home grown medication, and a comprehensive way to deal with residing as one with nature. The interconnectedness of these networks with their environmental factors is reflected in their ceremonies, legends, and everyday practices, all of which add to the conservation of the sensitive harmony among humankind and the climate.

One astounding part of nearby insight is its versatility. While certain components might appear to be customary or even old, they frequently develop to meet the changing necessities of the local area. This flexibility is a demonstration of the unique idea of neighborhood insight, which persistently coordinates new information while keeping up with its guiding principle. Along these lines, nearby insight fills in as an aide for exploring the intricacies of the cutting edge world while safeguarding the substance of social personality.

Direction from nearby insight reaches out past useful information to incorporate moral and moral standards. Numerous conventional social orders accentuate the significance of regard, collaboration, and correspondence. These qualities are in many cases imbued in day to day existence and are supported through stories, customs, and local area rehearses. By complying with these moral rules, people add to the prosperity of the local area overall, cultivating a feeling of solidarity and shared liability.

In certain societies, neighborhood shrewdness is sent through oral customs, with narrating assuming a focal part. Elderly folks act as the overseers of information, sharing stories that typify the aggregate insight of the local area. These accounts convey down to earth illustrations as well as act for of saving social legacy and building up a feeling of having a place. The passing down of oral practices guarantees that every age acquires the qualities, customs, and experiences that have supported the local area after some time.

Additionally, nearby insight frequently tracks down articulation in imaginative and imaginative structures. Conventional music, dance, and visual expressions act as mediums through which networks convey their set of experiences, values, and goals. These works of art are not simply improving yet are essential to the texture of day to day existence, giving a method for festivity, articulation, and correspondence. Through these imaginative outlets, nearby insight turns into a living, powerful power that adjusts to contemporary settings while holding its social importance.

Nearby direction stretches out to administration structures too, with numerous conventional social orders having laid out frameworks that focus on aggregate navigation and local area government assistance. The standards of inclusivity, agreement, and responsibility are implanted in these administration structures, guaranteeing that the requirements of the local area overshadow individual interests. Along these lines, neighborhood intelligence cultivates a feeling of social union and versatility, giving an establishment to maintainable and evenhanded turn of events.

Regardless of the wealth and strength of nearby insight, it isn't invulnerable to the difficulties presented by globalization and fast cultural changes. The disintegration of customary practices, the deficiency of native dialects, and the infringement of outside impacts can undermine the imperativeness of nearby insight. Perceiving and tending to these difficulties is essential for saving the variety of social legacy and guaranteeing that neighborhood shrewdness proceeds to direct and motivate people in the future.

One of the key difficulties confronting nearby insight is the effect of modernization on conventional practices. As people group take on new innovations and ways of life, there is a gamble of dismissing or forsaking respected traditions and information. The appeal of comfort and effectiveness related with present day practices can eclipse the more profound, frequently more slow, however more manageable methodologies implanted in nearby insight.

Language, being a transporter of social personality, assumes a critical part in the transmission of neighborhood shrewdness. The deficiency of native dialects is a grave worry, as it can prompt the vanishing of novel perspectives, communicating, and grasping the world. Endeavors to renew and protect native dialects are fundamental for defending the rich woven artwork of nearby insight that they exemplify.

Despite these difficulties, networks and people are progressively perceiving the significance of rejuvenating and advancing neighborhood insight. Endeavors to archive oral customs, support neighborhood craftsmans, and make instructive projects that incorporate conventional information into formal educational plans are picking up speed. These drives look for not exclusively to protect nearby insight yet additionally to feature its pertinence in tending to contemporary difficulties like natural maintainability, civil rights, and local area versatility.

One rousing illustration of the renewal of neighborhood astuteness is the developing interest in conventional environmental information (TEK). This information, established in the nearby cooperation among networks and their surroundings, offers important experiences into feasible asset the executives and biodiversity preservation. Perceiving the significance of TEK, a few preservation drives and logical examination projects currently effectively include neighborhood networks, recognizing their job as stewards of the land and storehouses of priceless biological insight.

Neighborhood direction likewise reaches out to the domain of wellbeing and prosperity. Numerous customary social orders have created refined frameworks of conventional medication that draw on neighborhood plants, minerals, and otherworldly practices. These all encompassing ways to deal with wellbeing address the actual side effects of ailment as well as the interconnectedness of brain, body, and soul. As interest in other option and integrative medication develops universally, there is a restored appreciation for the viability and shrewdness implanted in these conventional mending rehearses.

In addition, the standards of supportability inborn in neighborhood shrewdness are earning respect as fundamental commitments to the worldwide talk on ecological preservation. Customary horticultural practices, for example, agroforestry and permaculture, focus on the drawn out soundness of environments and soil fruitfulness. By embracing these tried and true methodologies, networks add to the protection of biodiversity and the moderation of environmental change, offering significant illustrations for practical farming for a bigger scope.

In the domain of schooling, there is a developing affirmation of the need to coordinate nearby insight into formal learning conditions. Instruction that integrates conventional information frameworks enhances the educational program as well as cultivates a deep satisfaction and character among understudies. Drives to foster socially applicable instructive materials, support native language training, and include local area seniors in the growing experience add to the protection and transmission of neighborhood shrewdness.

Taking everything into account, neighborhood astuteness and direction are significant resources that add to the variety, versatility, and manageability of networks all over the planet. As overseers of social legacy and vaults of down to earth and moral information, neighborhood shrewdness assumes an essential part in molding the character and prosperity of social orders. While confronting difficulties from modernization and globalization, endeavors to revive, safeguard, and advance nearby insight are significant for guaranteeing that this rich woven artwork of information proceeds to motivate and direct people in the future. Through a more profound comprehension and enthusiasm for nearby insight, we can fashion a more comprehensive and amicable way toward a common future.

5.1 The protagonist seeks guidance from local elders, shamans, or knowledgeable figures.

In the complex embroidery of human experience, the journey for direction from neighborhood seniors, shamans, or educated figures has been a perpetual subject across societies and ages. The hero, whether in a scholarly story or the unfurling show of reality, frequently sets out on an extraordinary excursion looking for the insight and experiences that main those well established in the customs and information on their local area can give.

Nearby elderly folks, loved for their gathered long stretches of involvement and shrewdness, assume a crucial part in molding the moral and moral compass of a local area. Their job goes past simply being vaults of verifiable information; they are living conductors of the aggregate ethos, epitomizing the qualities, customs, and social subtleties that characterize the personality of the local area. The hero, perceiving the meaning of this living repository of shrewdness, goes to these admired figures looking for direction that reaches out past the quick difficulties they face.

Shamans, frequently thought about go-betweens between the physical and otherworldly domains, carry an enchanted aspect to the journey for direction. Their insight stretches out past the unmistakable, including the concealed powers that impact the fates of people and networks. The hero, confronting existential quandaries or looking for bits of knowledge into the secrets of life, may search out these otherworldly aides. In the ethereal domain of the shaman's insight, the hero desires to find answers that rise above the ordinary and proposition a more profound comprehension of their motivation and spot in the great embroidery of presence.

Proficient figures inside a local area might incorporate elderly folks and shamans as well as people who have specific skill specifically spaces. These figures might be craftsmans, healers, or gatekeepers of explicit practices and specialties. Chasing direction, the hero perceives the significance of taking advantage of the different cluster of abilities and bits of knowledge that these people have. Whether looking for functional counsel, distinctive information, or mending expressions, the hero explores the multifaceted snare of local area ability to advance their own comprehension and capacities.

The demonstration of looking for direction from neighborhood older folks, shamans, or educated figures is established in a significant regard for the intergenerational move of shrewdness. In many societies, the transmission of information starting with one age then onto the next is a hallowed obligation, and the mentorship relationship is described by a profound feeling of correspondence. The hero, in moving toward these figures, recognizes the cooperative idea of this trade, understanding that the insight conferred isn't just for individual addition yet additionally to ultimately benefit the local area.

The direction looked for may take different structures — commonsense guidance for exploring the intricacies of day to day existence, moral lessons to explore moral problems, or profound bits of knowledge that rise above the limits of the material world. Elderly folks, with their abundance of life encounters, frequently share illustrations, stories, and maxims that embody ageless examples. The hero, mindful of the subtleties of these accounts, gathers experiences that act as directing lights in their own excursion.

Shamans, then again, may direct the hero through customs, services, or visionary encounters that rise above conventional awareness. The searcher, in the shamanic domain, may go through an emblematic passing and resurrection, acquiring a recharged point of view on their moves and a more profound association with the otherworldly components of presence. The direction got from a shamanic experience might be confounding, requiring translation and reflection with respect to the hero.

Proficient figures, whether craftsmans, healers, or experts in a specific field, offer a more substantial type of direction. The hero might acquire commonsense abilities, conventional specialties, or recuperating expressions that are essential to the local area's lifestyle. This involved apprenticeship grants explicit information as well as produces an association between the coach and the searcher, making a bond that stretches out past the simple exchange of data.

The mission for direction from nearby elderly folks, shamans, or proficient figures is in many cases outlined inside the setting of a transitional experience or a legend's excursion. The hero, at a pivotal point in their life, looks to rise above private limits, defeat preliminaries, and arise changed. This general account paradigm is reflected in fantasies, fables, and strict customs around the world, highlighting the immortal human requirement for mentorship, direction, and the groundbreaking force of astuteness.

During the time spent looking for direction, the hero might experience difficulties and tests that act as cauldrons for self-awareness. The coach, whether a senior, shaman, or proficient figure, may purposefully cause circumstances that push the limits of the searcher's usual range of familiarity. These difficulties are not simple impediments but rather open doors for the hero to exhibit versatility, boldness, and a reconciliation of the insight they have acquired.

The connection between the hero and the directing figures is dynamic, advancing after some time as the searcher incorporates the illustrations and intelligence bestowed. At first, the direction might be order, with the guide offering express directions and bits of knowledge. As the hero develops in their comprehension and encounters self-improvement, the relationship might move towards a more cooperative trade, where the searcher effectively draws in with the guide in an exchange of shared shrewdness.

It's fundamental to perceive that the direction looked for is definitely not a one-size-fits-all arrangement however a nuanced, setting subordinate interaction. The hero, as they continued looking for intelligence, should explore the social, social, and profound complexities of their local area. The direction got might be custom fitted to the particular difficulties and open doors that describe the hero's one of a kind excursion, making the cycle profoundly private and socially established.

In numerous stories and genuine situations, the direction looked for from nearby older folks, shamans, or educated figures is entwined with a more extensive subject of mutual interconnectedness. The hero's process isn't single however implanted in that frame of mind of the local area, and the insight acquired has repercussions past the person. The direction looked for isn't just for individual illumination yet for the more prominent prosperity of the system.

The social and profound legacy epitomized by nearby elderly folks, shamans, and educated figures fills in as an establishing force in the midst of commotion and change. As people group wrestle with the effect of modernization, globalization, and moving cultural standards, the direction from these respected figures turns into a balancing out force. The hero, by looking for and exemplifying this insight, turns into an extension between the past and the future, adding to the congruity and flexibility of their social personality.

The direction looking for venture isn't without its intricacies and ambiguities. The hero might experience clashing counsel, moral situations, or the test of incorporating apparently divergent types of intelligence. These strains are intrinsic to the human experience and mirror the diverse idea of direction. The searcher should explore the maze of viewpoints, knowing the more deeply insights that resound with their own qualities and the requirements of their local area.

In the domain of writing and narrating, the theme of looking for direction from neighborhood seniors, shamans, or learned figures is a common subject across sorts. From the legend's excursion in legendary stories to the bildungsroman in transitioning stories, the hero's journey for shrewdness fills in as a story framework that rises above social limits.

Writers, drawing on the aggregate oblivious, weave stories that reverberate with perusers by taking advantage of the general human longing for direction and self-disclosure.

In non-fictitious records, the genuine journey for direction frequently reflects the prototype accounts tracked down in writing. People confronting critical life advances, existential emergencies, or moral junction might go to tutors, profound aides, or local area pioneers for experiences that rise above tried and true way of thinking. These stories, whether fictitious or grounded as a general rule, highlight the immortal importance of the direction looking for venture as an extraordinary and enlightening cycle.

The depiction of direction looking for in different social and strict practices further highlights its importance as a widespread human encounter. In strict accounts, prophets and profound pioneers frequently set out on excursions of disclosure, looking for divine direction that shapes the predetermination of their networks. The model of the savvy senior or savvy, present in fantasies and legends, represents the immortal allure of looking for astuteness from the people who have navigated the ways of life previously.

The direction looking for venture isn't restricted to conventional or native societies; it reverberates with people in contemporary society wrestling with the intricacies of current life. In a time set apart by fast mechanical headways, social disturbances, and ecological difficulties, the requirement for direction from sources well established in social insight turns out to be considerably more articulated. The hero, whether exploring the intricacies of an influencing world or grappling with inward devils, looks for the immortal insights that rise above fleeting and spatial limits.

5.2 Discover the wisdom passed down through generations about the mystical elements of Majestic Heights.

In the quieted murmurs of Superb Levels, an embroidery of mystery unfurls, woven with strings of old insight went down through ages. Magnificent Levels, where the ethereal and natural merge, holds mysteries that rise above time. The people group, settled between transcending tops and hidden in a quality of charm, isn't just a geological area yet a storehouse of otherworldly components that have molded the existences of its occupants for a really long time.

The mysterious components of Great Levels are unpredictably associated with the normal scene that supports the local area. Older folks, narrators, and caretakers of custom have, over ages, woven accounts that instill each slope, stream, and tree with profound importance. The passing down of these stories is a consecrated obligation, guaranteeing that the pith of Great Levels is saved in the shared perspective of its kin.

At the core of Grand Levels' magic is a significant love for the land and its cycles. The changing seasons are meteorological events as well as impressions of grandiose powers that impact the recurring pattern of life.

Older folks, with endured faces and eyes that have seen the dance of innumerable seasons, are the narrators who disclose the mysteries of the land. Through oral customs, they give information about the meaning of each season, the energies they bring, and the ceremonies that blend with nature's rhythms.

The great pinnacles that embrace Magnificent Levels are not simple land arrangements but rather respected substances with characters and accounts of their own. Older folks retell stories of the old watchmen who live on these pinnacles, looking after the local area with considerate eyes. These gatekeepers, it is expressed, convey through the stirring leaves, the murmuring breezes, and the delicate influence of branches. The occupants, receptive to these normal discoursed, figure out how to decipher the unobtrusive messages implanted in the components, looking for direction and knowledge.

Water, streaming in translucent streams that navigate the scene, is a holy course in Grand Levels' enchantment. Seniors tell stories of the Water Spirits, watchmen of immaculateness and essentialness, staying in the secret openings of flowing cascades. Customs related with water, performed with accuracy and respect, are accepted to lay out a sacrosanct association with these spirits, guaranteeing the local area's prosperity. The passing down of these customs is a hallowed demonstration, restricting every age to the existence force that courses through Magnificent Levels.

The vegetation of Lofty Levels are not simply natural elements but rather transporters of imagery and intelligence. Trees, viewed as old sentinels, are viewed as vessels of tribal spirits. Elderly folks describe how certain trees are blessed with the recollections of the individuals who have left, and communing with these arboreal seniors turns into a custom of recognition. The magical meaning of plants reaches out to herbalism, where information on restorative properties is gone down through apprenticeships, making a heredity of healers who grasp the speculative chemistry of nature.

In the core of Great Levels lies a hallowed woods, a safe-haven where the cloak between the natural and otherworldly domains is supposed to be meager. Elderly folks guide the more youthful ages to this woods, starting them into the unobtrusive craft of communing with the concealed. Customs acted in this hallowed space are permeated with the pith of extraordinary energies, cultivating a profound association with the otherworldly aspects that shape the predeterminations of the people who call Great Levels home.

The heavenly domain, with its stars, heavenly bodies, and infinite dance, is one more aspect of Great Levels' supernatural quality. Older folks, with eyes that have thought about the night sky for a really long time, are divine guides, disentangling the messages written in the examples of stars.

The passing down of divine legend incorporates the specialty of mysterious understanding, where the developments of superb bodies are viewed as signs directing choices and activities. The skies, in Glorious Levels, are very easy to read of enormous insight read by the people who look for bits of knowledge past the earthly domain.

Customs and services in Glorious Levels are not simple exhibitions but rather living articulations of the supernatural components that shape the local area's character. Seniors arrange these customs, implanting them with the reverberation of genealogical voices and the beat of the land. Each signal, each serenade, and each offering is a string in the mind boggling embroidery of Lofty Levels' otherworldliness, associating the past, present, and future in an immortal dance of profound congruity.

The passing down of magical information in Grand Levels includes verbal transmission as well as experiential learning. Inceptions into the secrets of the land frequently appear as journeys to hallowed locales, where the searcher goes through soul changing experiences that stir lethargic faculties and open passages to the concealed. Older folks, as guides in these excursions, become channels for the exchange of profound energy, working with an immediate association between the searcher and the magical components of Glorious Levels.

Dreams, seen as entrances to the psyche and profound domains, hold an extraordinary spot in Superb Levels' magic. Seniors are respected as translators of dreams, having the capacity to unwind the representative language that winds through the woven artwork of the evening. The direction got from dreams isn't inconsistent yet is viewed as a type of divination, offering looks into the secret flows of fate. The passing down of dream translation abilities guarantees that this old workmanship stays a living practice, a wellspring of understanding for the individuals who explore the cryptic scenes of the psyche.

Magnificent Levels' supernatural quality isn't restricted to the bounds of individual encounters; it pervades the collective awareness. Celebrations, celebrated with extravagance and gravity, are an outflow of aggregate appreciation, worship, and satisfaction. Elderly folks, as overseers of the hallowed schedule, organize these celebrations, adjusting them to divine occasions, occasional changes, and the recurrent rhythms of nature. The collective ceremonies, set apart by dance, music, and representative establishments, act as a mutual fellowship with the otherworldly powers that shape the fate of Great Levels.

The supernatural components of Magnificent Levels are not resistant to the unyielding walk of time and the undeniable trends. As outer impacts enter the hallowed territory, there is a fragile equilibrium to be kept up with between saving custom and adjusting to the developing necessities of the local area.

Older folks, as watchmen of the magical heritage, face the test of exploring this sensitive balance, guaranteeing that the quintessence of Grand Levels' supernatural quality perseveres while embracing the open doors introduced by the unfurling present.

The passing down of otherworldly information in Magnificent Levels includes a hallowed pledge between ages. Elderly folks, in sharing the mysteries of the land, endow the more youthful individuals from the local area with the obligation of leading of mystery forward. This transmission isn't one-sided; it is a complementary trade where the liveliness of youth meets the carefully prepared insight old enough. The intergenerational exchange guarantees that the magical components of Lofty Levels stay a no nonsense power that adjusts to the developing necessities of the local area.

Notwithstanding modernization, Lofty Levels' supernatural quality fills in as a signal, helping its occupants to remember their underlying foundations and the interconnectedness between the seen and the concealed. Elderly folks, as torchbearers of custom, guide the local area in exploring the intricacies of contemporary life while saving the holy strings that tight spot them to the magical embroidered artwork of their legacy. The supernatural components, a long way from being relics of the past, become wellsprings of motivation and versatility notwithstanding change.

The enchantment of Lofty Levels is definitely not a confined peculiarity yet part of a more extensive embroidery that winds around together the profound customs of different societies around the world. The equals between the enchanted components of Great Levels and those found in different customs highlight the general human journey for association with the sacrosanct and the otherworldly. Elderly folks, as the stewards of this general insight, become spans between the neighborhood and the worldwide, cultivating a feeling of connection with searchers from far off lands who reverberate with the otherworldly call of Grand Levels.

All in all, the supernatural components of Magnificent Levels, went down through ages, comprise a living embroidery of shrewdness that entwines the otherworldly and the earthly. Older folks, as the overseers of this mystery, assume a fundamental part in sending the insider facts of the land, the heavenly legend, and the holy customs that characterize the local area's personality. The supernatural excursion in Superb Levels is certainly not a single undertaking yet a public investigation, a dance of ages that guarantees the immortal congruity of the sacrosanct strings woven into the actual texture of the magnificent scene. As the unavoidable trends murmur through Great Levels, the enchantment perseveres, a consistently present aide for the individuals who look to explore the concealed domains and find the persevering through insight of the ages.

5.3 Develop relationships between the protagonist and the community.

In the multifaceted dance of story, the connections between the hero and the local area act as a dynamic and critical component. The interaction among individual and group, formed by shared encounters, customs, and goals, winds around a rich embroidery that adds profundity and intricacy to the hero's excursion. Whether set in the striking scenes of fiction or repeating the rhythms of genuine networks, the bonds produced between the hero and the aggregate substance around them contribute essentially to the unfurling story.

At the core of these connections is the hero's association with the local area's social texture. The people group, with its customs, esteems, and shared history, turns into a supply from which the hero draws food and personality. The embroidery of aggregate memory, gave over through ages, entwines with the hero's very own account. Older folks, narrators, and the aggregate oral practice act as extensions between the at various times, connecting the hero to the tribal roots that anchor them locally's common legacy.

The shared story isn't only a background yet a functioning member in the hero's excursion. The hero, formed by the tales and shrewdness went down through ages, conveys the shared mindset of the local area inside them. Thusly, the hero's activities, decisions, and encounters become strings woven into the continuous story, affecting the common predetermination of the local area. This equal relationship makes a harmonious dance among individual and aggregate stories, each impacting and improving the other.

The hero's introduction into the local area frequently includes transitional experiences, representative services, or common festivals. These customs, profoundly implanted locally's social embroidered artwork, mark the hero's coordination into the aggregate character. Whether it's a transitioning function, a collective celebration, or a common ceremony that means acknowledgment, these customs fashion a connection between the hero and the local area, securing them in a common story of having a place and reason.

The connections inside the local area stretch out past simple acquaintanceship; they structure a snare of reliance that characterizes the hero's emotionally supportive network. Family, companions, tutors, and, surprisingly, the puzzling figures prowling behind the scenes all add to the hero's development and flexibility. The people group turns into a mosaic of different characters, each assuming a novel part in the hero's excursion. From the direction of elderly folks to the fellowship of friends, these connections offer the hero an organization of profound, social, and at times even otherworldly help.

Struggle, an intrinsic part of any story, tracks down reverberation inside the connections of the local area. The hero, exploring the intricacies of relational elements, should wrestle with conflicts, misconceptions, and once in a while even disloyalty.

These struggles, however testing, act as cauldrons for the hero's personality advancement. The goal of relational strains inside the local area turns into a subplot that reflects the more extensive bend of the hero's excursion, offering experiences into the complexities of human association.

In the cauldron of shared difficulties, the connections between the hero and the local area go through extraordinary cycles. Difficulty turns into an impetus for solidarity, strength, and the manufacturing of more profound associations. The hero's battles become symbolic of the aggregate battle, and their triumphs resound with the victories of the local area. The common encounters of difficulty make a mutual story of flexibility, encouraging a feeling of fortitude and mutual perspective among the occupants of the local area.

Correspondence, both verbal and non-verbal, assumes an essential part in forming connections inside the local area. The hero, as a communicator, should explore the subtleties of discourse, exchange, and understanding. Language, with its nuances and social implications, turns into a scaffold or an obstruction in the connections between the hero and the different individuals from the local area. The capacity to convey successfully, to tune in and be heard, turns into an expertise that impacts the direction of the hero's connections.

The hero's process frequently includes the mentorship of older folks or prepared individuals from the local area. These guide mentee connections become channels for the exchange of shrewdness, abilities, and social information. Elderly folks, with their abundance of involvement, act as guides, giving functional experiences as well as moral and moral lessons. The mentorship dynamic turns into a story string that winds through the hero's development, adding to their development inside the mutual setting.

The people group, as a powerful element, develops close by the hero. The hero's activities, choices, and the results of their decisions echo through the shared mindset of the local area. The account bend of the local area, impacted by the hero's excursion, mirrors the harmonious connection among individual and aggregate predeterminations. As the hero faces difficulties, goes through private change, or accomplishes achievements, the local area, as well, goes through shifts that reflect the more extensive cultural elements at play.

The rhythmic movement of connections inside the local area are affected by the hero's adherence to or deviation from cultural standards and values. The strain between individual cravings and collective assumptions turns into a story support, moving the hero into moral difficulties, moral situations, and thoughtful excursions. decisions by the hero echo through the texture of the local area, starting conversations, discusses, and some of the time even social movements inside the aggregate mind.

The hero's connections inside the local area stretch out past the human circle to incorporate the normal world. The climate, with its verdure, fauna, and scenes, turns into a quiet observer to the hero's excursion. The people group's association with nature frequently shapes its social practices, customs, and perspective. The hero's relationship with the regular components turns into a similitude for their association with the more extensive local area and the infinite powers that impact their fate.

The hero's excursion locally is certainly not a direct direction however a repeating dance of takeoff and return. The story beat incorporates times of investigation, self-revelation, and outer difficulties, trailed by periods of homecoming, gathering, and shared festivals. Each re-visitation of the local area denotes another section in the hero's relationship with the group, as well as a chance for the local area to observe and recognize the development and changes gone through by the hero.

In the connections between the hero and the local area, the subject of personality becomes the overwhelming focus. The hero's singular personality is unpredictably entwined with their public character. The investigation of selfhood, molded by mutual assumptions, social legacy, and individual yearnings, turns into a focal story circular segment. The people group, as both a mirror and a pot, mirrors the hero's developing self-appreciation and assumes an essential part in the hero's journey for character and reason.

As the hero's process unfurls, the idea of having a place turns into a strong subject in their associations with the local area. The requirement for acknowledgment, understanding, and a feeling of home shapes the hero's communications with the aggregate substance around them. Whether the local area fills in as a safe-haven or a wellspring of contention, the hero's mission for a spot inside the public embroidery turns into a main thrust that impels the story forward.

The connections inside the local area are not static; they develop, mature, and once in a while conflict over the long haul. The hero, as a powerful power inside the local area, goes through self-awareness that resounds through their connections with others. Fellowships extend, familial bonds are tried and reinforced, and the hero's job inside the collective elements shifts because of the difficulties and disclosures of their excursion.

The hero's associations with the local area may likewise include the investigation of social variety inside the public setting. In people group that envelop a mosaic of identities, customs, and conviction frameworks, the hero's process turns into a diverse investigation. Exploring the subtleties of social trade, beating generalizations, and cultivating figuring out become necessary parts of the hero's connections inside this assorted local area.

Classified or furtive connections inside the local area add layers of intricacy to the story. Secret partnerships, secret social orders, or implicit associations become story components that contribute interest, tension, and a feeling of secret to the connections inside the local area.

The hero's disclosure of these hid elements turns into a story impetus that pushes them more profound into the complexities of the mutual embroidery.

The connections inside the local area may likewise be molded by outside impacts, like cultural changes, financial movements, or political disturbances. The people group turns into a microcosm mirroring the more extensive socio-social scene, and the hero's connections should explore the flows of progress that move throughout both individual lives and the aggregate element. The interchange between the hero and the local area turns into a focal point through which cultural changes are noticed and deciphered.

In the woven artwork of connections, clashes emerge from relational elements as well as from the conflict of individual longings with public assumptions. The hero, as a harbinger of progress, may challenge laid out standards, question customs, or defy foundational treacheries inside the local area. The subsequent strains become account circular segments that investigate the sensitive harmony between individual organization and aggregate union.

The connections inside the local area frequently interweave with subjects of adoration and sentiment. Whether exploring the intricacies of familial assumptions, cultural standards, or prohibited wants, the hero's heartfelt snares become basic features of their connections inside the local area. Love, as both a wellspring of satisfaction and a possible wellspring of contention, adds profound profundity to the common story.

Treachery, a strong story gadget, may appear inside the connections of the local area. The hero's confidence in companions, guides, or even relatives might be tried, prompting impactful snapshots of break and compromise. The investigation of double-crossing inside the mutual setting adds layers of profound intricacy to the account, moving the hero to face the delicacy of trust inside the obligations of local area.

The connections inside the local area frequently track down goal or change through mutual get-togethers and festivities. Celebrations, functions, and shared customs become central focuses that tight spot the hero to the aggregate element. These collective occasions act as pots for profound therapy, compromise, and the reaffirmation of shared values, stamping vital minutes in the hero's excursion.

The connections between the hero and the local area unfurl against the scenery of the local area's physical and topographical climate. The scenes, milestones, and holy spaces become observers to the hero's victories, preliminaries, and changes. The normal setting, with its excellence and difficulties, reflects the recurring pattern of the hero's connections inside the local area, making a cooperative energy between the inner and outer elements of the story.

As the connections inside the local area develop, the story investigates the subject of inheritance. The hero's activities, decisions, and effect on the local area make a permanent imprint on the aggregate character. The passing down of customs, information, and the hero's story turns into a type of social legacy, molding the fate of the local area for a long time into the future.

All in all, the connections between the hero and the local area comprise a nuanced and dynamic embroidery that winds around together individual stories with aggregate predeterminations. Whether set against the background of fiction or repeating the rhythms of genuine networks, these connections add profundity, intricacy, and close to home reverberation to the hero's excursion. The exchange between the hero and the local area turns into a story dance, a cooperative investigation of character, having a place, and the persevering through bonds that shape the mutual embroidery.

In the multifaceted dance of story, the connections between the hero and the local area act as a dynamic and essential component. The interchange among individual and group, molded by shared encounters, customs, and desires, winds around a rich embroidery that adds profundity and intricacy to the hero's excursion. Whether set in the clear scenes of fiction or repeating the rhythms of genuine networks, the bonds fashioned between the hero and the aggregate element around them contribute fundamentally to the unfurling account.

At the core of these connections is the hero's association with the local area's social texture. The people group, with its practices, esteems, and shared history, turns into a supply from which the hero draws food and character. The embroidery of aggregate memory, gave over through ages, entwines with the hero's very own account. Elderly folks, narrators, and the aggregate oral custom act as scaffolds between the over a wide span of time, connecting the hero to the tribal roots that anchor them locally's common legacy.

The public story isn't only a background yet a functioning member in the hero's excursion. The hero, formed by the accounts and shrewdness went down through ages, conveys the shared perspective of the local area inside them. Thusly, the hero's activities, decisions, and encounters become strings woven into the continuous story, affecting the common fate of the local area. This corresponding relationship makes a harmonious dance among individual and aggregate stories, each impacting and improving the other.

The hero's introduction into the local area frequently includes soul changing experiences, emblematic services, or public festivals. These ceremonies, profoundly implanted locally's social embroidery, mark the hero's coordination into the aggregate personality. Whether it's a transitioning service, a mutual celebration, or a common custom that implies acknowledgment, these ceremonies manufacture a connection between the hero and the local area, mooring them in a common story of having a place and reason.

The connections inside the local area stretch out past simple acquaintanceship; they structure a trap of reliance that characterizes the hero's emotionally supportive network. Family, companions, tutors, and, surprisingly, the cryptic figures hiding behind the scenes all add to the hero's development and flexibility. The people group turns into a mosaic of different characters, each assuming a one of a kind part in the hero's excursion. From the direction of elderly folks to the kinship of friends, these connections offer the hero an organization of close to home, social, and once in a while even otherworldly help.

Struggle, an innate part of any story, tracks down reverberation inside the connections of the local area. The hero, exploring the intricacies of relational elements, should wrestle with conflicts, misconceptions, and now and again even disloyalty. These struggles, however testing, act as pots for the hero's personality improvement. The goal of relational pressures inside the local area turns into a subplot that reflects the more extensive circular segment of the hero's excursion, offering experiences into the complexities of human association.

In the cauldron of shared difficulties, the connections between the hero and the local area go through extraordinary cycles. Misfortune turns into an impetus for solidarity, flexibility, and the manufacturing of more profound associations. The hero's battles become symbolic of the aggregate battle, and their triumphs resound with the victories of the local area. The common encounters of difficulty make a mutual story of versatility, encouraging a feeling of fortitude and common perspective among the occupants of the local area.

Correspondence, both verbal and non-verbal, assumes an essential part in molding connections inside the local area. The hero, as a communicator, should explore the subtleties of exchange, discussion, and understanding. Language, with its nuances and social undertones, turns into an extension or a hindrance in the connections between the hero and the different individuals from the local area. The capacity to convey successfully, to tune in and be heard, turns into an expertise that impacts the direction of the hero's connections.

The hero's process frequently includes the mentorship of older folks or prepared individuals from the local area. These guide mentee connections become conductors for the exchange of astuteness, abilities, and social information. Elderly folks, with their abundance of involvement, act as guides, bestowing reasonable experiences as well as moral and moral lessons. The mentorship dynamic turns into a story string that winds through the hero's development, adding to their development inside the common setting.

The people group, as a unique element, develops close by the hero. The hero's activities, choices, and the outcomes of their decisions echo through the shared awareness of the local area. The story circular segment of the local area, affected by the hero's excursion, mirrors the advantageous connection among individual and aggregate fates. As the hero faces difficulties, goes through private change, or accomplishes achievements, the local area, as well, goes through shifts that reflect the more extensive cultural elements at play.

The recurring pattern of connections inside the local area are affected by the hero's adherence to or deviation from cultural standards and values. The pressure between individual longings and collective assumptions turns into a story support, moving the hero into moral situations, moral issues, and contemplative excursions. decisions by the hero echo through the texture of the local area, starting conversations, discusses, and some of the time even social movements inside the aggregate mind.

The hero's connections inside the local area reach out past the human circle to incorporate the regular world. The climate, with its verdure, fauna, and scenes, turns into a quiet observer to the hero's excursion. The people group's association with nature frequently shapes its social practices, ceremonies, and perspective. The hero's relationship with the normal components turns into an illustration for their association with the more extensive local area and the enormous powers that impact their fate.

The hero's excursion locally is certainly not a direct direction yet a recurrent dance of flight and return. The story mood incorporates times of investigation, self-revelation, and outer difficulties, trailed by periods of homecoming, get-together, and mutual festivals. Each re-visitation of the local area denotes another section in the hero's relationship with the group, as well as a chance for the local area to observe and recognize the development and changes gone through by the hero.

In the connections between the hero and the local area, the topic of character becomes the dominant focal point. The hero's singular character is complicatedly joined with their collective personality. The investigation of selfhood, formed by common assumptions, social legacy, and individual desires, turns into a focal story circular segment. The people group, as both a mirror and a cauldron, mirrors the hero's developing self-appreciation and assumes a vital part in the hero's journey for character and reason.

As the hero's process unfurls, the idea of having a place turns into a piercing subject in their associations with the local area. The requirement for acknowledgment, understanding, and a feeling of home shapes the hero's connections with the aggregate substance around them. Whether the local area fills in as a safe-haven or a wellspring of contention, the hero's mission for a spot inside the mutual embroidery turns into a main impetus that moves the story forward.

The connections inside the local area are not static; they advance, mature, and now and again conflict over the long haul. The hero, as a powerful power inside the local area, goes through self-awareness that resonates through their cooperations with others. Companionships extend, familial bonds are tried and fortified, and the hero's job inside the common elements shifts because of the difficulties and disclosures of their excursion.

The hero's associations with the local area may likewise include the investigation of social variety inside the common setting. In people group that envelop a mosaic of identities, customs, and conviction frameworks, the hero's process turns into a multifaceted investigation. Exploring the subtleties of social trade, conquering generalizations, and encouraging grasping become necessary parts of the hero's connections inside this different local area.

Secret or undercover connections inside the local area add layers of intricacy to the account. Secret collusions, secret social orders, or implicit associations become story components that contribute interest, tension, and a feeling of secret to the connections inside the local area. The hero's disclosure of these hid elements turns into a story impetus that pushes them more profound into the complexities of the shared embroidery.

The connections inside the local area may likewise be formed by outer impacts, like cultural changes, monetary movements, or political disturbances. The people group turns into a microcosm mirroring the more extensive socio-social scene, and the hero's connections should explore the flows of progress that move throughout both individual lives and the aggregate element. The exchange between the hero and the local area turns into a focal point through which cultural changes are noticed and deciphered.

In the embroidered artwork of connections, clashes emerge from relational elements as well as from the conflict of individual cravings with collective assumptions. The hero, as a harbinger of progress, may challenge laid out standards, question customs, or face fundamental treacheries inside the local area. The subsequent pressures become story curves that investigate the fragile harmony between individual organization and aggregate union.

The connections inside the local area frequently interlace with topics of adoration and sentiment. Whether exploring the intricacies of familial assumptions, cultural standards, or taboo cravings, the hero's heartfelt snares become basic aspects of their connections inside the local area. Love, as both a wellspring of bliss and a likely wellspring of contention, adds profound profundity to the shared story.

Treachery, an intense story gadget, may appear inside the connections of the local area. The hero's confidence in companions, tutors, or even relatives might be tried, prompting powerful snapshots of burst and compromise. The investigation of double-crossing inside the mutual setting adds layers of close to home intricacy to the story, provoking the hero to defy the delicacy of trust inside the obligations of local area.

The connections inside the local area frequently track down goal or change through mutual social events and festivities. Celebrations, functions, and shared ceremonies become central focuses that tight spot the hero to the aggregate substance. These collective occasions act as cauldrons for close to home therapy, compromise, and the reaffirmation of shared values, checking significant minutes in the hero's excursion.

The connections between the hero and the local area unfurl against the setting of the local area's physical and geological climate. The scenes, milestones, and hallowed spaces become observers to the hero's victories, preliminaries, and changes. The regular setting, with its excellence and difficulties, reflects the rhythmic movement of the hero's connections inside the local area, making a cooperative energy between the inward and outer elements of the story.

As the connections inside the local area advance, the story investigates the topic of heritage. The hero's activities, decisions, and effect on the local area make a permanent imprint on the aggregate personality. The passing down of customs, information, and the hero's story turns into a type of social legacy, molding the fate of the local area for a long time into the future.

All in all, the connections between the hero and the local area comprise a nuanced and dynamic embroidery that winds around together individual stories with aggregate fates. Whether set against the scenery of fiction or repeating the rhythms of genuine networks, these connections add profundity, intricacy, and profound reverberation to the hero's excursion. The exchange between the hero and the local area turns into a story dance, a cooperative investigation of character, having a place, and the persevering through bonds that shape the collective embroidery.

Chapter 6

Facing Challenges

In the tremendous embroidery of human life, confronting difficulties is an unavoidable and essential part of the excursion. Life unfurls in capricious ways, giving people a horde of deterrents that test their strength, versatility, and mettle. These difficulties come in different structures, enveloping the domains of individual, proficient, and cultural aspects. The human experience is a powerful interchange among wins and hardships, and exploring through misfortune frequently characterizes one's way of living.

At the individual level, people wrestle with subtle conflicts and outer tensions that shape their personality and manufacture their character. The excursion of self-disclosure is loaded with vulnerabilities and intricacies, expecting people to stand up to their most profound apprehensions, instabilities, and vulnerabilities. The journey for self-understanding requests reflection and the eagerness to go up against awkward insights. An interaction unfurls over the long haul, set apart by snapshots of disclosure and mindfulness.

Additionally, individual connections contribute essentially to the woven artwork of difficulties that people experience. Communications with family, companions, and significant others give pleasure and satisfaction, however they additionally present intricacies and clashes. Correspondence breakdowns, varying qualities, and the recurring pattern of feelings make many-sided snare of challenge inside the domain of human connections. The capacity to explore these difficulties with sympathy, understanding, and viable correspondence is fundamental for encouraging solid associations.

In the expert circle, people are faced with a scene of chances and impediments that shape their vocations and add to their expert development. The serious idea of the cutting edge work environment requests flexibility and a nonstop obligation to expertise improvement. Progressions in innovation, changes in market elements, and changes in industry patterns require a proactive way to deal with vocation the executives.

Work related difficulties reach out past the outside factors influencing ventures and markets. Working environment elements, workplace issues, and relational contentions present extra layers of intricacy. Finding some kind of harmony among desire and coordinated effort, emphaticness and lowliness, is a fragile dance that experts should dominate. Exploring through the complexities of office culture and hierarchical orders requires the capacity to understand individuals on a profound level, flexibility, and an essential mentality.

Cultural difficulties, then again, rise above the individual and the expert, incorporating more extensive issues that influence networks, countries, and the worldwide populace. Cultural difficulties can appear in different structures, including monetary aberrations, political flimsiness, natural emergencies, and social treacheries. Tending to these difficulties requires aggregate activity, a common feeling of obligation, and a pledge to cultivating good change.

Financial difficulties, like destitution and pay imbalance, make obstructions to individual and aggregate advancement. The inconsistent dissemination of assets and open doors sustains a pattern of hindrance for minimized networks. Handling monetary difficulties requires fundamental changes, strategies that advance inclusivity, and a deliberate work to overcome any barrier between the wealthy and the poor.

Political difficulties, described by administration issues, defilement, and international strains, have expansive results on a worldwide scale. The intricacies of worldwide relations and the fragile overall influence among countries add to a steadily developing scene of political difficulties. Building discretionary scaffolds, advancing discourse, and encouraging worldwide participation are basic for tending to these difficulties and advancing worldwide solidness.

Natural difficulties, set apart by environmental change, deforestation, and contamination, represent a danger to the actual groundwork of human life. The outcomes of ecological debasement reach out past public lines, affecting environments and weak networks around the world.

Relieving these moves requires an aggregate obligation to supportable practices, preservation endeavors, and a principal shift in the manner in which humankind connects with the climate.

Social difficulties, established in separation, imbalance, and bad form, endure regardless of progress in different regions. Bigotry, sexism, and different types of bias keep on tormenting social orders, ruining the acknowledgment of genuine balance. Defying social difficulties requires a change in outlook in cultural perspectives, regulative measures to safeguard minimized gatherings, and a promise to destroying foundational obstructions that sustain separation.

Notwithstanding these diverse difficulties, people and networks frequently end up at an intersection, constrained to go with decisions that will shape their fates. The excursion of confronting difficulties is definitely not a straight way however a perplexing and dynamic course of development and variation. It requires an eagerness to embrace distress, gain from disappointments, and develop strength notwithstanding misfortune.

One of the major parts of confronting difficulties is the attitude with which people approach them. A development mentality, instead of a decent outlook, is portrayed by the conviction that capacities and insight can be created through commitment and difficult work. Embracing a development mentality enables people to see difficulties as any open doors for learning and development as opposed to inconceivable impediments.

The excursion of confronting difficulties is many times joined by a scope of feelings, including dread, uncertainty, and uneasiness. These feelings are regular reactions to the vulnerabilities inborn in facing the unexplored world. Recognizing and handling these feelings is an essential move toward building profound strength. It requires a readiness to face distress, investigate the main drivers of these feelings, and foster survival techniques to explore through them.

Besides, the capacity to develop flexibility is a foundation of confronting difficulties really. Versatility isn't the shortfall of affliction however the ability to return from mishaps, adjust to change, and drive forward even with challenges. Building versatility includes fostering an encouraging group of people, cultivating a positive mentality, and gaining from the two triumphs and disappointments. It is a ceaseless course of fortifying one's capacity to endure the hardships of life.

Versatility is one more key part of effectively confronting difficulties. The capacity to adjust to evolving conditions, turn when essential, and embrace advancement empowers people to explore through vulnerability effortlessly. In a quickly developing world, flexibility is a significant expertise that enables people to flourish in different conditions and jump all over new chances that might emerge.

In the domain of individual difficulties, the excursion of self-disclosure is much of the time a groundbreaking cycle. It includes investigating one's qualities, interests, and reason throughout everyday life. The mission for self-disclosure expects people to face their apprehensions, question cultural assumptions, and manufacture their own way. A profoundly private excursion unfurls over the long haul, set apart by breakthrough moments, mindfulness, and self-awareness.

Exploring through the complexities of individual connections is a continuous test that requires compelling correspondence, sympathy, and a pledge to common development. Correspondence breakdowns, clashes, and developing elements request a proactive way to deal with building and supporting solid connections. Developing capacity to appreciate anyone on a profound level, grasping alternate points of view, and rehearsing undivided attention are fundamental abilities in the perplexing embroidery of human associations.

Inside the expert scene, the difficulties people face are just about as different as the professions they seek after. The quest for progress and satisfaction in the expert domain requires an essential way to deal with objective setting, consistent learning, and flexibility. Whether ascending the professional bureaucracy, exploring the intricacies of business venture, or seeking after an inventive undertaking, experts experience a scope of difficulties that shape their expert personality.

Office elements, portrayed by progressive systems, group connections, and authoritative culture, present the two open doors and difficulties. Really exploring through the complexities of the working environment requires a mix of initiative abilities, the capacity to understand people on a deeper level, and a cooperative outlook. Offsetting desire with modesty, confidence with tact, experts should develop a flexible range of abilities to flourish in the cutthroat scene of the advanced working environment.

Besides, profession challenges reach out past the limits of the individual and meet with more extensive financial patterns, innovative headways, and industry elements. Remaining significant in a quickly advancing proficient scene requires a pledge to deep rooted learning, versatility, and a proactive way to deal with expertise improvement. The capacity to expect and answer changes in the gig market is a basic part of effectively confronting proficient difficulties.

Cultural difficulties, traversing monetary, political, ecological, and social aspects, are perplexing and interconnected. Tending to these difficulties requires aggregate activity, a common feeling of obligation, and a promise to cultivating good change. People, people group, and countries should team up to make practical arrangements that rise above restricted interests and advance the prosperity of the worldwide populace.

Financial difficulties, like destitution and pay disparity, request a thorough and comprehensive way to deal with monetary turn of events. This includes carrying out approaches that focus on evenhanded circulation of assets, admittance to schooling and medical services, and potential open doors for monetary portability. Furthermore, encouraging business and development can add to making a more strong and versatile economy that helps a more extensive range of society.

Political difficulties, portrayed by administration issues, debasement, and international strains, require strategic endeavors, global collaboration, and a pledge to maintaining popularity based standards. Building solid foundations, advancing straightforwardness, and tending to the underlying drivers of political shakiness are fundamental stages in conquering these difficulties. The worldwide local area should cooperate to guarantee harmony, strength, and the security of common liberties on a worldwide scale.

Natural difficulties, driven by environmental change, deforestation, and contamination, require an aggregate obligation to manageable practices and preservation endeavors. People, organizations, and legislatures should focus on natural stewardship, embrace green advancements, and work towards diminishing fossil fuel byproducts. Worldwide drives and global collaboration are essential in relieving the effect of ecological difficulties and safeguarding the planet for people in the future.

Social difficulties, established in segregation, disparity, and shamefulness, require a complex way to deal with advance social union and uniformity. Authoritative measures that safeguard underestimated gatherings, instructive drives that advance variety and incorporation, and grassroots developments that challenge prejudicial standards are essential parts of tending to social difficulties. Cultivating sympathy, understanding, and a pledge to civil rights are fundamental in building a more evenhanded society.

Despite these difficulties, versatility, flexibility, and a proactive outlook become principal. The capacity to explore through misfortune, whether at the individual, proficient, or cultural level, requires a blend of inward strength and outer help. Building versatility includes developing a positive mentality, creating survival strategies, and gaining from encounters, both positive and negative.

Versatility, the ability to conform to evolving conditions, empowers people and networks to flourish in powerful conditions. Embracing change as a chance for development, instead of a danger, engages people to explore through vulnerability with certainty. The difficulties of life, however imposing, become impetuses for change and self-revelation when met with versatility and strength.

Additionally, cooperation and aggregate activity are basic to tending to difficulties that stretch out past the person. In the interconnected universe of the 21st hundred years, worldwide difficulties require worldwide arrangements. Cooperative endeavors between countries, associations, and people are fundamental in handling issues, for example, environmental change, monetary imbalance, and international pressures. Building spans, encouraging exchange, and advancing a feeling of shared liability are urgent in making an additional agreeable and economical world.

Taking everything into account, confronting difficulties is an inborn piece of the human experience. The excursion of standing up to individual, proficient, and cultural difficulties is a perplexing and dynamic interaction that shapes people and networks. The capacity to explore through misfortune requires a mix of inward strength, flexibility, and a proactive mentality.

Individual difficulties, set apart by the excursion of self-revelation and the intricacies of human connections, request contemplation, compassion, and a promise to self-improvement. Proficient difficulties, established in the serious scene of the cutting edge working environment, require nonstop learning, versatility, and an essential way to deal with profession improvement. Cultural difficulties, including financial, political, natural, and social aspects, call for aggregate activity, global collaboration, and a pledge to encouraging positive change.

Even with these difficulties, people and networks have the chance to develop versatility, embrace flexibility, and add to a superior world. The embroidered artwork of human life is woven with strings of wins and adversities, and it is currently confronting difficulties that the genuine substance of life is uncovered. As people explore through the intricacies of their excursions, they have the ability to shape their fates, add to the prosperity of others, and leave a persevering through heritage for people in the future.

6.1 The protagonist encounters challenges and trials on their quest.

Leaving on a mission is a groundbreaking excursion that unfurls in the embroidery of a hero's life, winding around together difficulties and preliminaries that shape their personality and fate. The actual embodiment of a mission lies in the burdensome way the hero should cross, loaded up with snags that test their guts, versatility, and assurance. A story prime example rises above social limits, resounding through fantasies, legends, and writing, showing the general idea of the human experience and the legend's excursion.

As the hero sets out on their journey, they are many times driven by a convincing reason or a call to experience. This call fills in as the impetus that drives them into the obscure, pushing them past the solace of the natural and into the domain of vulnerability. The excursion, nonetheless, is certainly not a direct way yet rather a tangled odyssey set apart by difficulties that act as cauldrons of change.

The difficulties experienced on the journey are multi-layered, going from outer foes to unseen fits of turmoil that reflect the hero's internal battles. Outer difficulties can appear as considerable adversaries, deceptive scenes, or outlandish deterrents that stand between the hero and their objective. These outside foes serve as actual obstacles as well as representations for the hero's own apprehensions, questions, and impediments.

Preliminaries of actual ability frequently accentuate the legend's excursion, requesting the hero's solidarity, expertise, and cleverness. Whether engaging legendary animals, exploring tricky territories, or conquering apparently impossible chances, the actual difficulties highlight the legend's assurance and ability. It is through these preliminaries that the hero finds the profundities of their own true capacity and the flexibility that lives inside.

Nonetheless, the legend's process stretches out past the actual domain, diving into the complexities of the hero's mind. Unseen fits of turmoil, like self-question, moral predicaments, and the showdown of individual devils, add layers of intricacy to the mission. These interior difficulties are many times more subtle and significant than outside foes, requiring the hero to face their own weaknesses and explore the maze of their own mind.

The experience with coaches and partners assumes a vital part in the legend's excursion, giving direction, shrewdness, and backing to the hero. These tutors, frequently model figures, add to the legend's development and advancement by granting information, sharing experiences, and testing their suppositions. The connections fashioned with partners become a wellspring of solidarity and kinship, offering the hero comfort in the midst of misfortune.

However, the legend's process isn't without snapshots of isolation and thoughtfulness. The hero should wrestle with snapshots of detachment, overcoming their own feelings of dread and vulnerabilities without the solace of friendship. It is in these lone minutes that the legend faces the real essence of their journey and gains a more profound comprehension of themselves.

The topic of penance is complicatedly woven into the texture of the legend's excursion. Whether it be private penances, surrendering solace and security for everyone's best interests, or confronting the deficiency of valued connections, the journey requests an eagerness to persevere through difficulty and pursue hard choices. The penances made by the hero highlight the respectability of their objective and the profundity of their obligation to the mission.

As the hero advances on their excursion, they frequently experience emblematic limits and final turning points. These significant minutes mark advances in the account, implying the legend's development and the irreversible idea of their decisions. Passing the boundary addresses a takeoff from the common world and a pledge to the remarkable, driving the hero further into the unexplored world.

The idea of change is fundamental to the legend's excursion. The difficulties and preliminaries looked by the hero are not only outside snags but rather impetuses for self-awareness and transformation. The legend goes through a course of self-revelation, shedding the layers of their previous self to uncover a more enabled, edified, and developed person. The actual excursion turns into a pot, producing the hero into a legend fit for defying their fate.

Even with difficulty, the hero should gather an unflinching determination to continue on. The dauntless soul inside them fills in as a directing light through the most obscure corners of their mission. The legend's process is a demonstration of the human limit with respect to strength, showing that, even despite inconceivable chances, the human soul can persevere, adjust, and at last victory.

The journey, nonetheless, is certainly not a direct direction yet a recurrent and recursive example. Similarly as the hero vanquishes one bunch of difficulties, they are pushed into new preliminaries that request further development and change. The repeating idea of the legend's process mirrors the unending journey for personal growth and the consistent quest for higher standards.

The goal of the legend's process frequently comes full circle in the achievement of their objective or the acknowledgment of their motivation. This goal isn't just an outside win yet an impression of the inside transformation gone through by the hero. The mission, completely, fills in as a story illustration for the legend's inward excursion — an excursion that rises above time, culture, and individual conditions.

The persevering through allure of the legend's process lies in its comprehensiveness and ageless reverberation. It addresses the human condition, epitomizing the substance of battle, win, and self-revelation. The difficulties and preliminaries looked by the hero reflect the difficulties that people experience in their own lives, making a story system that welcomes thoughtfulness and self-reflection.

In writing, folklore, and film, endless instances of the legend's process flourish. From the mythic missions of old legends like Odysseus and Ruler Arthur to the contemporary accounts of characters like Frodo Baggins and Harry Potter, the legend's process takes on assorted structures, adjusting to the social and topical subtleties of various stories. This flexibility highlights the persevering through pertinence and flexibility of the legend's excursion as a story paradigm.

Past its story importance, the legend's process fills in as an illustration for the human quest for significance and reason. The mission turns into an emblematic portrayal of the singular's excursion through life, with its heap difficulties and groundbreaking minutes. It urges people to embrace their own chivalrous potential, perceiving that inside each individual lies the limit with regards to mental fortitude, strength, and the quest for a reason more significant than oneself.

All in all, the hero's experience with difficulties and preliminaries on their journey is a story model that rises above social, worldly, and individual limits. The legend's excursion, woven into the texture of human narrating, mirrors the general idea of the human experience. As the hero explores the maze of their mission, confronting outside enemies, unseen struggles, and snapshots of isolation, they go through a course of change that shapes their personality and characterizes their predetermination. The legend's process is a demonstration of the unstoppable soul inside each individual — a soul that can persevere, adjust, and win even with difficulty. Whether in old legends or contemporary stories, the legend's process proceeds to enrapture and motivate, welcoming people to leave on their own journeys of self-revelation, development, and the quest for a specific reason that rises above the customary.

6.2 Develop tension and suspense as they navigate through difficult terrain or face adversaries.

The air balanced weighty with pressure as the heroes wandered into the core of the disallowing territory, a scene that appeared to oppose all their means. The climate was thick with a dismal quietness, broken exclusively by the far off wail of the breeze and the stirring of concealed animals in the shadows. As they explored through the troublesome territory, vulnerability gripped to them like a cover, every footfall repeating the heaviness of the difficulties that lay ahead.

The actual landscape appeared to scheme against them — a maze of curved ways, twisted roots, and forcing rock developments that remained as quiet sentinels, protecting the mysteries hid inside. The very ground underneath their feet appeared to move, making an agitating feeling of unsteadiness. With each step, they felt the substantial pressure, a premonition mindfulness that the excursion ahead held risks yet concealed.

Not set in stone and fearless, pushed on through the unforgiving scene. The landscape tried their actual perseverance as well as their psychological strength. Each diversion in the way appeared to be intended to muddle them, a purposeful endeavor to plant the seeds of uncertainty to them. The tension constructed consistently as they confronted the tireless test of exploring through a maze that seemed to have its very own psyche.

As they dug further, a feeling of segregation settled upon the heroes — an inclination that they were entering a domain immaculate by time, where the principles of the standard world presently not applied. The scary tranquility was periodically broken by the far off calls of concealed animals, adding a component of concealed enemies prowling in the shadows. The strain uplifted with each shadow that glinted at the fringe of their vision, leaving them anxious, uncertain of what looked for them in the dimness.

It was not just the landscape that represented a danger. Foes, shrewd and slippery, prowled in the shadows, keeping a close eye on them. The heroes could detect the look of inconspicuous eyes, an imperceptible presence that appeared to expect all their means.

The tension developed as they turned out to be very much in the know that they were in good company — an acknowledgment that powered their assurance yet in addition elevated their weakness.

The experiences with foes were inconsistent however extreme, every showdown leaving a waiting feeling of disquiet. The foes, whether humanoid or supernatural, appeared to have an uncanny comprehension of the heroes' shortcomings. The tension worked as the heroes confronted enemies that were essentially as mysterious as the actual landscape, their intentions darkened by a cloak of secret. The heroes were passed on to puzzle over whether these enemies were simple snags or part of a bigger, coordinated challenge that looked for them.

The heroes, energized by a mix of boldness and franticness, took part in a sensitive hit the dance floor with their enemies. Each experience was a trial of mind and expertise, a high-stakes game where the outcomes posed a potential threat. The tension arrived at its pinnacle as the heroes explored through a tricky dance of methodology and avoidance, never knowing when the following enemy would rise up out of the shadows.

Amidst this hazardous excursion, the heroes ended up wrestling with outside dangers as well as with struggles under the surface. The tension of the territory and the steady quest for enemies stressed the obligations of brotherhood, taking steps to disentangle the solidarity that had been their solidarity. The tension extended as the heroes stood up to the difficulties that lay before them as well as the breaks inside their own gathering, a gap that, whenever left unattended, could demonstrate more damaging than any outer foe.

The actual components appeared to scheme against the heroes, strengthening the tension as time passes. The sky, when a material of blue serenity, obscured with inauspicious mists that accumulated not too far off. The weather conditions turned into an unstable power, switching back and forth between searing intensity and frigid virus. The heroes confronted not just the malice of the territory and foes yet in addition the flighty fury of nature — a power that additional an eccentric layer to the generally problematic excursion.

Exploring through troublesome territory and confronting foes turned into a tireless cycle, a progression of pinnacles and valleys that reflected the close to home and actual cost for the heroes. The tension was not only an outer develop but rather an unavoidable propensity that invaded each part of their excursion. It turned into a no nonsense element, looped around them like a snake, its presence felt in the fixing of their chests and the enlivening of their breath.

As the heroes approached the perfection of their journey, the pressure arrived at a breaking point. The excursion had turned into a cauldron, manufacturing them into a new thing, something fashioned in the pot of misfortune. The tension was as of now not simply a setting; it turned into the actual texture of their reality, woven into the embroidery of their aggregate insight.

Each step, each choice, turned into a snapshot of uplifted expectation, as though the actual universe paused its breathing, holding back to perceive how the heroes would explore the last, definitive difficulties.

The peak of the excursion unfurled in a crescendo of tension — a climax of the multitude of preliminaries, hardships, and enemies that had characterized their journey. The heroes remained at the limit of their definitive objective, an award that gleamed with the commitment of satisfaction and disclosure. However, the tension waited, a waiting vulnerability about whether the excursion had genuinely reached a conclusion or on the other hand in the event that there stayed one last contort in the story.

The goal of the tension was not a simple uncovering of the objective but rather a disclosure of the significant changes that had happened inside the heroes. The troublesome landscape and enemies had not only been outside hindrances; they had been impetuses for transformation. The heroes arose out of the pot of their excursion not as similar people who had left upon it yet as developed creatures, molded and sharpened by the difficulties they had confronted.

The outcome, however an arrival of pressure, was not a re-visitation of the common. The heroes, everlastingly different, conveyed the reverberations of their excursion inside them. The tension, while settled, left an enduring engraving — an update that the actual excursion was essentially as huge as the objective. The troublesome landscape and foes had not been enemies in the customary sense; they had been guides, pushing the heroes past their apparent cutoff points and into the domain of the remarkable.

Truth be told, the story of exploring through troublesome landscape and confronting enemies is a nuanced dance between outside difficulties and inward changes. The tension that penetrates the excursion is definitely not a simple scholarly gadget yet an impression of the significant vulnerabilities and intricacies innate in the human experience. It is a demonstration of the strength of the human soul, the unyielding will to push forward in any event, when confronted with apparently unrealistic chances. As the heroes explore through the maze of their mission, the tension turns into a mirror held up to the peruser's own excursion — an encouragement to defy difficulties, explore vulnerabilities, and arise changed on the opposite side.

6.3 Highlight the resilience and determination of the protagonist.

The hero, a solitary figure remaining at the very front of their own story, arises as a signal of flexibility and assurance. From the beginning of their excursion, a resolute purpose establishes the vibe for the difficulties and preliminaries that will follow. This dauntless soul moves them forward, a power that won't respect the difficulties that lie ahead.

As the hero sets out on their journey, the actual pith of their personality is characterized by an internal strength that turns out to be progressively clear with every snag confronted. The excursion unfurls not as a comfortable walk around the unremarkable but rather as a persistent odyssey requesting the greatest possible level of backbone.

Whether crossing troublesome landscape or facing considerable enemies, the hero's versatility is a steady friend, an immaterial covering that safeguards them against the turbulent flows of their journey.

The troublesome landscape turns into an imposing foe by its own doing, a persistent power that looks to challenge and test the constraints of the hero's perseverance. The scene, set apart by deceptive ways, unforgiving geology, and flighty components, fills in as a figurative milestone. However, despite such misfortune, the hero's assurance focuses as a directing light. Each step, regardless of how difficult, turns into a demonstration of their responsibility, a confirmation that they won't be dissuaded by the difficulties that nature itself has tossed in their way.

The territory, however apparently unconcerned with the battles of the hero, turns into a cauldron for the fashioning of their strength. The components plot to establish a threatening climate, exposing the hero to the singing intensity of a tireless sun or the gnawing chill of unforgiving breezes. However, in the midst of the brutality of their environmental elements, the hero continues. The assurance to vanquish the troublesome landscape isn't energized by a longing for solace however by an inborn need to survive, to demonstrate that the human soul can win over the most brutal of conditions.

It is at the times of isolation, where the hero is left to battle with the huge scope of the landscape and the reverberations of their own strides, that their strength really comes to the front. The forlornness of the excursion turns into a material whereupon the hero paints their steady responsibility. Without even a trace of outer approval or friendship, the inward fire of assurance keeps the hero pushing forward, a fire that will not be quenched by the tremendous vacancy that stretches before them.

Enemies, both seen and inconspicuous, arise as imposing difficulties on the hero's excursion. Whether as outer enemies or struggles under the surface, the hero's strength turns into an intense weapon against the powers that try to block their advancement. The foes might take on horde structures — a guile foe, a legendary animal, or the shadows of their own questions. However, the hero's assurance stays resolute, a revitalizing cry that reverberations despite resistance.

In the experiences with foes, the hero's flexibility isn't just a safeguard however a weapon sharpened by the discharge of their own internal battles. The fights, whether physical or mental, become fields for the displaying of their unfaltering soul.

It isn't the shortfall of dread or vulnerability that characterizes the hero however their capacity to defy these feelings head-on, to recognize the difficulties before them and push forward in spite of the approaching apparition of difficulty.

The actual pith of assurance is enlightened in the decisions the hero makes when confronted with enemies. There is a cognizant choice to stand up to as opposed to sidestep, to figure out the difficulties with an enduring look. This readiness to draw in with difficulty changes the hero's excursion into a confirmation of flexibility. The story isn't an account of evasion or avoidance yet a narrative of confronting difficulties with a fortitude that will not be stifled.

The versatility of the hero stretches out past simple actual ability. It turns into a quality that pervades each feature of their being — their considerations, their feelings, and their communications with the world. In snapshots of weakness, when uncertainty takes steps to create a shaded area over their way, the hero's assurance turns into a directing power. A reference point slices through the haziness of vulnerability, enlightening a way ahead in any event, when the objective remaining parts darkened.

Partners and guides, while offering priceless help, likewise act as mirrors mirroring the hero's versatility. The connections produced along the way turned into a demonstration of the strength of the hero's personality. The bonds shaped are not based on a groundwork of delicacy but rather on the persevering through nature of assurance. The partners observer firsthand the immovable responsibility of the hero, and thusly, their own purpose is fortified by the unyielding soul they track down in the hero's organization.

The isolation of the excursion, however set apart by snapshots of reflection and self-revelation, doesn't decrease the hero's association with their own strength. In snapshots of segregation, when the heaviness of the mission pushes ahead upon them, the hero's assurance fills in as a sidekick — a resolute partner that murmurs support in the quiet. It is this inward discourse, the steady self-insistence of direction, that supports the hero through the most obscure snapshots of the excursion.

As the hero advances, the story unfurls not as a straight walk but rather as a powerful hit the dance floor with difficulty. The strength showed is definitely not a static characteristic however a no nonsense power that adjusts to the changing scenes of the mission. The difficulties confronted, whether physical, close to home, or existential, become open doors for the hero to advance, to refine their assurance in the pot of involvement.

The account bend arrives at its pinnacle in the climactic snapshots of the excursion. The goal of the mission isn't simply the fulfillment of an objective yet the zenith of the hero's change. The versatility that once filled in as a safeguard has now turned into a necessary piece of their personality. The assurance, tried and refined through the pot of difficulties, is presently not a particular power yet a core value that will shape the hero's future undertakings.

In the outcome, the repercussions of the hero's excursion, the story doesn't close with a feeling of resoluteness however with the acknowledgment that flexibility and assurance are persevering through characteristics. The hero, having beaten the hardships, conveys the reverberations of their excursion into the unexplored world. The mission might have arrived at its decision, yet the unyielding soul that characterized the hero's personality keeps on consuming splendidly — a fire that will light the way through the unfamiliar domains that lie ahead.

All in all, the story of the hero exploring through troublesome landscape and confronting foes is an orchestra of versatility and assurance. From the initial step of the excursion to the perfection of the mission, the hero's enduring determination fills in as the foundation of their personality. It's anything but a static quality yet a unique power that adjusts and develops with each challenge confronted. The story turns into a demonstration of the persevering through nature of the human soul, a festival of the unstoppable will that won't be quenched by the preliminaries of the journey. Through the hero's excursion, the peruser is welcome to observe the extraordinary force of strength and assurance — a power that rises above the limits of the story and resounds as a persevering through reverberation in the aggregate human experience.

At the core of each and every convincing story lies the unyielding assurance of the hero — an unflinching power that impels them through the complexities of their excursion, controlling them through the rhythmic movement of difficulties, and eventually characterizing the direction of their personality circular segment. This perseverance isn't simply a scholarly gadget; it is a dynamic, throbbing energy that reinvigorates the all hero's activities, choice, and conflict with misfortune.

From the beginning of the hero's excursion, assurance appears as the main impetus that moves them into the unexplored world. The call to experience, whether a murmur on the breeze or a booming thunder, is met with an undaunted choice to set out on the journey. This underlying flash of assurance denotes the beginning of the hero's odyssey — a promise to cross unfamiliar regions, defy considerable enemies, and unwind the secrets that lie ahead.

The excursion unfurls against a scenery of difficulties that act as cauldrons, testing the fortitude of the hero's assurance. Troublesome territory, with its unforgiving scenes and slippery ways, turns into a material whereupon the hero's flexibility is painted. The assurance to push forward, undaunted by the snags that nature tosses their direction, changes the troublesome landscape from a simple actual landmark into an otherworldly field where the hero's solidarity of will is sharpened.

Each step taken, each obstacle conquered, is a demonstration of the hero's unflinching determination. The troublesome landscape, with its exciting bends in the road, turns into a mirror mirroring the steadfast responsibility of the hero. Whether scaling transcending tops or exploring thick woodlands, assurance turns into the compass directing them through the maze of difficulties. Not the shortfall of snags characterizes the excursion however the hero's steady assurance to vanquish them.

The scene, however not interested in the battles of the hero, takes on an emblematic importance. It turns into a mirror mirroring the hero's own inside scene — the pinnacles and valleys of their feelings, the exciting bends in the road of their viewpoints. In exploring through the actual difficulties of troublesome landscape, the hero is likewise exploring the complicated territory of their own mind. Assurance turns into a directing light, enlightening the way through the outside and interior wild similar.

Enemies, tricky and considerable, arise as impressive difficulties on the hero's excursion. These foes are not simple outside snags; they are indications of the struggles that live inside the hero. The assurance to defy these enemies head-on, to participate in the multifaceted dance of technique and battle, turns into a characterizing element of the hero's personality. The fights are not battled for triumph alone yet as a sign of the hero's faithful obligation to their mission.

The experiences with enemies are not absent any and all snapshots of uncertainty or dread. It is the assurance to confront these feelings, to recognize them without surrendering to their incapacitating grasp, that hoists the hero's strength. Every enemy, whether a shadowy figure in the evening or a considerable enemy on the combat zone, turns into a cauldron for the hero's assurance. The fights are battled with weapons as well as with an unshakeable confidence in the honorableness of the journey.

Partners and tutors, while offering help and direction, likewise become observers to the hero's assurance. The connections manufactured along the way are not simple partnerships but rather impressions of the hero's personality. Assurance turns into an attractive power that draws close friends, fashioning bonds that rise above the difficulties confronted. The partners become friends in-arms, partaking in the triumphs and losses, and seeing the dauntless soul that characterizes the hero.

The isolation of the excursion, however set apart by snapshots of contemplation and self-revelation, doesn't lessen the hero's association with their own assurance. In snapshots of confinement, when the boundlessness of the journey poses a potential threat, assurance turns into an inward exchange — a tireless self-certification of direction. The hero, remaining at the nexus of their own considerations, draws strength from this inward well of assurance, a well that won't dry up even in that frame of mind of significant isolation.

As the hero explores the maze of their journey, assurance arises as a receptive power as well as a proactive aide. It is the driving energy behind the hero's choices, the power that constrains them to face challenges, make forfeits, and oppose the chances. Assurance is definitely not an inactive quality ready to be tried; a functioning power shapes the actual forms of the story.

The strength of the hero stretches out past actual ability. It turns into a quality that saturates each feature of their being — their considerations, their feelings, and their communications with the world.

In snapshots of weakness, when uncertainty takes steps to create a shaded area over their way, the hero's assurance turns into a directing power. A signal slices through the murkiness of vulnerability, enlightening a way ahead in any event, when the objective remaining parts darkened.

The story circular segment arrives at its apex in the climactic snapshots of the excursion. The goal of the mission isn't only the fulfillment of an objective however the zenith of the hero's change. The assurance that once filled in as a safeguard has now turned into an essential piece of their personality. The fights, whether physical or mental, have not just been challenges of solidarity however pots for the producing of a strong will.

In the conclusion, the fallout of the hero's excursion, the story doesn't finish up with a feeling of resoluteness however with the acknowledgment that assurance is a persevering through quality. The hero, having defeated the hardships, conveys the reverberations of their excursion into the unexplored world. The mission might have arrived at its decision, yet the unyielding soul that characterized the hero's personality keeps on consuming splendidly — a fire that will light the way through the unknown domains that lie ahead.

All in all, the story of the hero's assurance is an orchestra of flexibility and unwavering purpose. From the call to experience to the summit of the journey, assurance fills in as the hero's steady friend. It's anything but a uninvolved quality however a powerful power that adjusts, develops, and shapes the actual texture of the story. Through the hero's excursion, the peruser is welcome to observe the extraordinary force of assurance — a power that rises above the bounds of the story and resounds as a persevering through reverberation in the aggregate human experience.

Chapter 7

Revelation at the Summit

At the break of sunrise, as the principal beams of daylight painted the sky in tints of pink and gold, a solitary figure climbed the precarious, winding way that prompted the highest point. The air was fresh, and a delicate breeze murmured through the old trees that lined the path. Birds twittered their morning tunes, unaware of the weight that laid on the shoulders of the solitary voyager.

The excursion had been long and burdensome, set apart by difficulties and preliminaries that tried the constraints of perseverance. However, every step had been a cognizant decision, a guarantee to arrive at the zenith of an excursion that held the commitment of disclosure. The highest point, darkened by the fog that gripped to the levels, appeared to entice with a quiet confirmation of significant information anticipating revelation.

As the explorer moved toward the highest point, the air developed more slender, and the environmental factors changed into a strange scene of rocks and inadequate vegetation. The world beneath was covered in an ocean of mists, and the far off pinnacles of adjoining mountains rose like old sentinels watching the mysteries of the levels.

With each step, the explorer's heart beat in a state of harmony with the musicality of the excursion, a demonstration of the steady quest for a reality that had evaded the grip of customary humans. The way was steep, and the climb requested actual strength, yet a significant versatility of soul. It was a journey of the spirit, a mission for grasping that rose above the limits of the material world.

After arriving at the highest point, the explorer stopped to pause and rest. The view that unfurled before them was absolutely striking. The world underneath appeared to be far off and unimportant, a simple bit in the immense material of presence. The culmination, presently washed in the warm shine of the morning sun, uncovered itself as a sacrosanct space where the standard met the remarkable.

As the explorer remained on the highest point, a significant quietness wrapped the environmental elements. Maybe time itself had stopped to observe the perfection of an excursion that spread over actual distance, however the profundities of internal investigation. The disclosure looked for was not in that frame of mind of the view or the separation of the levels however in the calm openings of the explorer's own cognizance.

At that time of quietness, the voyager shut their eyes, permitting the vibes of the culmination to saturate each fiber of their being. The breeze conveyed murmurs of antiquated intelligence, and the stones underneath their feet appeared to hold the recollections of ages past. It was a fellowship with the components, an acknowledgment of the interconnectedness, everything being equal.

As the explorer woke up, a dream unfurled before them. A figure, brilliant and ethereal, showed up at the edge of the culmination. It exuded a presence that rose above the physical, an indication of a cognizance that stretched out past the restrictions of mortal presence.

"Good tidings, searcher of truth," the ethereal figure talked, its voice resounding with a melodic congruity that appeared to resonate through the actual texture of the real world.

The voyager, lowered by the presence before them, answered, "Who are you, and what information do you hold?"

"I'm the attendant of the highest point, the gatekeeper of disclosures," the figure answered. "The information you look for isn't a belonging to be gotten a handle on however a comprehension to be embraced. The acknowledgment of the solidarity ties all life, the mindfulness that rises above the deceptions of detachment."

With these words, the figure broadened a hand, and a surge of light moved from its fingertips. In a moment, the explorer was wrapped in an outpouring of pictures and sensations. It was an excursion through reality, a brief look into the embroidery of presence that wove together the strings of creation.

The explorer saw the introduction of stars and the dance of worlds, the rhythmic movement of seas, and the development of life on far off planets. They saw civic establishments rise and fall, each influencing the shared perspective of the universe. It was a disclosure that rose above the limits of uniqueness, uncovering an immense interconnected trap of presence.

As the dreams unfurled, the explorer felt a significant feeling of unity with the universe. The limits of self broke down, and they turned into an observer to the infinite show that worked out across the immense spread of the real world. It was an acknowledgment that each experience, each bliss and distress, was a string in the unpredictable embroidery of presence.

Once more, the ethereal figure talked, "The disclosure you look for isn't bound to this culmination however is an impression of the timeless reality that lives inside you. It is the acknowledgment that the actual excursion is the objective, and each step taken with expectation and care is a stage toward edification."

The explorer, presently drenched in a condition of uplifted mindfulness, felt a profound feeling of appreciation for the direction got. The culmination, when seen as the endpoint of a mission, changed into a representative edge prompting a higher comprehension.

As the ethereal figure disappeared, the explorer plunged from the culmination, conveying with them the disclosures that rose above the limits of the actual world. The plummet, however a re-visitation of the natural landscape, was instilled with a freshly discovered clearness and reason.

With each step, the explorer assimilated the insight acquired at the culmination. It was not information to be stored however a fire to be shared, a reference point of enlightenment to direct others on their excursions of self-revelation. The disclosure at the culmination was not an end but rather a start, an impetus for a daily existence lived with expectation and a profound association with the pith of presence.

The world underneath, once far off and unnoticeable, presently unfurled with a recharged energy. Each collaboration, each second, turned into a valuable chance to communicate the disclosures woven into the texture of the voyager's being. The excursion proceeded, not as a direct movement but rather as a never-ending investigation of the limitless potential outcomes that lay implanted in the embroidery of presence.

In the valleys and fields, in the midst of the clamoring urban communities and calm towns, the explorer turned into a living demonstration of the groundbreaking force of disclosure. Through words and activities, they shared the insight acquired at the highest point, lighting the flash of interest and self-revelation in those they experienced.

The disclosures, similar to swells in a tremendous grandiose lake, spread outward, contacting the existences of people and networks. The searcher of truth had turned into a harbinger of progress, an impetus for an aggregate arousing that rose above the constraints of existence.

As the voyager traveled through the embroidered artwork of presence, they experienced individual searchers on their own excursions. The trading of stories and encounters turned into an embroidery inside the bigger woven artwork, a meshing together of individual strings into an orchestra of interconnected lives.

The disclosures at the highest point were not static yet powerful, developing with every collaboration and experience. The voyager, presently an aide and an ally to other people, embraced the smoothness of the excursion. The highest point, when a particular objective, turned into a representation for the consistent unfurling of understanding and the endless layers of truth ready to be found.

The explorer's way converged with different scenes - the dry deserts of difficulties, the prolific fields of development, and the thick timberlands of thoughtfulness. Every landscape offered its own arrangement of examples, and the explorer explored with strength and elegance, drawing upon the disclosures carved into their cognizance.

In the organization of close allies, the explorer tracked down comfort and motivation. Together, they shaped a local area of searchers, joined by the ongoing idea of a common journey for truth. The trading of thoughts and viewpoints improved the aggregate comprehension, making an embroidery of variety inside the bigger embroidery of solidarity.

As the seasons changed and years passed, the explorer saw the repetitive idea of presence. Birth and demise, satisfaction and distress, creation and disintegration - each period of the excursion held its own importance in the terrific arrangement of life. The disclosures, once significant and dazzling, presently appeared in the effortlessness of regular minutes.

The explorer, presently enhanced with the patina of astuteness, kept on traveling through the always changing scene of presence. The culmination, however ancient history, stayed a directing light, a sign of the timeless realities that rose above the transient idea of the material world.

In snapshots of quietness, the explorer would shut their eyes and return to the highest point in the openings of their cognizance. The ethereal figure, presently a piece of their inward scene, kept on offering direction and consolation. The disclosures, similar to a wellspring of motivation, streamed unendingly, recharging the explorer's obligation to a daily existence lived with reason and care.

As the explorer matured, their actual structure went through the unavoidable course of progress. However, the soul stayed strong, an everlasting fire that consumed splendidly in the midst of the fleeting dance of the components. The disclosures, presently woven into the actual texture of the explorer's being, turned into a wellspring of solace and strength notwithstanding life's unavoidable difficulties.

In the sundown of their reality, the voyager got back to the culmination one final time. A truly epic excursion, presently a round trip, conveyed the heaviness of encounters and the lavishness of a spirit that had navigated the profundities of self-disclosure. The culmination, washed in the delicate shine of dusk, appeared to invite the fatigued voyager back to where everything started.

As the explorer remained on the highest point, a feeling of fruition washed over them. The disclosures, once looked for with intense assurance, had turned into a fundamental piece of their character. The ethereal figure, presently a quiet presence inside, gestured in affirmation.

"Searcher of truth, you have embraced the disclosures and led of intelligence through the embroidery of presence," the ethereal figure talked, its voice a delicate murmur conveyed by the night breeze. "The culmination was nevertheless a mirror mirroring the insights that dwell inside. Your process go on past the bounds of existence."

With a heart brimming with appreciation, the voyager offered a quiet goodbye to the culmination. The drop, presently a re-visitation of the infinite dance of presence, held the commitment of fresh starts. The disclosures, presently an inheritance to be passed on, kept on reverberating through the passageways of the voyager's cognizance.

Thus, the excursion unfurled, not as a direct movement but rather as a ceaseless investigation of the boundless potential outcomes that lay implanted in the embroidery of presence. The disclosures at the culmination, however profoundly private, had risen above the limits of independence, turning into an immortal orchestra that resounded with the heartbeat of the universe.

As the explorer blurred into the records of time, their story turned into a piece of the aggregate story of searchers who had stepped the way of self-disclosure. The disclosures at the highest point, similar to a signal in the tremendous span of presence, kept on directing the people who considered leaving on the excursion of revealing the secrets that lay inside.

In the excellent embroidery of life, every searcher, similar to a string, added to the complex winding of a story that rose above the limits of reality. The disclosures at the highest point were not restricted to a particular second but rather reverberated through the ages, a demonstration of the timeless mission for understanding and the getting through soul of the human spirit.

Thus, the highest point remained as a quiet observer to the endless excursions that unfurled in its shadow. Searchers would travel every which way, each transforming the consecrated space of disclosure. The ethereal figure, a watchman and guide, stayed a steady presence, an exemplification of the all inclusive bits of insight that rose above the back and forth movement of mortal presence.

In the huge grandiose dance, the disclosures at the culmination were nevertheless a solitary note in an orchestra that spread over the limitlessness of creation. The embroidered artwork of presence, steadily changing and forever advancing, kept on winding around together the accounts of endless searchers who, in their quest for truth, found the immortal insight that dwelled inside the profundities of their own being.

Thus, the highest point, washed in the everlasting light of grasping, remained as a demonstration of the ceaseless excursion of self-revelation. The disclosures, similar to a hallowed fire, copied brilliantly in the hearts of the people who thought for even a moment to climb the levels and look into the limitless field of probability. The tale of the searcher, the culmination, and the disclosures reverberated through the hallways of time, an everlasting song that blended with the vast rhythms of presence.

7.1 The climax of the story occurs as the protagonist reaches the summit of Kilimanjaro.

In the core of East Africa, where the huge savannah loosens up underneath the overwhelming look of Mount Kilimanjaro, an excursion of self-disclosure unfurled. The hero, driven by an inward calling, left on a mission that rose above the actual scene and dove into the profundities of their own spirit. Kilimanjaro, with its glorious pinnacle hidden in mists, remained as the representative edge where the peak of this significant story would unfurl.

The excursion had not been a simple one. It was a journey across the untamed wild, exploring the maze of prickly shrubs and crossing the undulating territory. The hero's strides reverberated as one with the musical beats of the African wild, where the air was thick with the fragrances of earth and life.

As the rising proceeded, the air developed more slender, and the environmental factors changed into a supernatural scene. The natural hints of the savannah gave way to the quieted murmurs of the mountain winds, and the vegetation became meager, giving looks at the rough landscape underneath. The trip was not only an actual undertaking; it was an otherworldly odyssey, a journey to the culmination where disclosures anticipated.

The hero, filled by an unyielding soul, proceeded, each stage a demonstration of the flexibility of the human spirit. The mountain, a quiet observer to innumerable stories carved into its rough façade, appeared to coax the hero with an ethereal charm. The peak of the story was not just about arriving at the actual pinnacle of Kilimanjaro however about opening the inward sanctum of oneself.

At the foundation of the culmination, weakness weighed intensely on the hero's appendages, and uncertainty cast its shadow across their determination. However, the call from the levels was faithful, an alarm's melody that reverberated through the tremendous breadth. With each step, the hero faced the inward devils that looked to hinder their advancement - questions, fears, and the reverberations of past injuries.

The excursion reflected the changes of life, with snapshots of win and battle, satisfaction and despondency. It was a microcosm of the human experience, revealed against the fantastic material of Kilimanjaro's inclines. As the hero climbed, the layers of oneself were stripped away, uncovering the crude pith underneath. The culmination, however still far off, lingered as an image of trust and change.

As the height expanded, the air turned out to be meager, and the environmental elements transformed into a dreamlike dreamscape. The sun cast long shadows on the rough shakes, and the hero's breath turned into a noticeable demonstration of the difficulties confronted. The excursion, when set apart by the energetic shades of the savannah, presently unfurled in shades of dark and white, an unmistakable difference to the distinctiveness of the world underneath.

As time passes, the hero felt an unobtrusive change in cognizance. The trip became an actual undertaking as well as a similitude for the climb to higher conditions of mindfulness. The highest point, hidden in fog and secret, addressed the peak of the hero's mission for importance, where the limits between oneself and the universe would obscure.

As the culmination moved close to, a significant tranquility settled upon the scene. Maybe time itself paused its breathing, expecting the finish of an excursion that crossed the domains of the seen and the concealed. The hero, presently at the doorstep of the highest point, felt a flood of feelings - a blend of expectation, stunningness, and a significant feeling of achievement.

The last push to the highest point was a significant hardship and will. Each step felt heavier, yet the call from the levels was an undetectable tie, pulling the hero vertical. The mountain, with its transcending precipices and fissure, turned into a similitude for life's difficulties, and the culmination, a token of the versatility that lives inside the human soul.

Finally, with the sun hanging low not too far off, providing reason to feel ambiguous about a warm shine the rough surface, the hero remained on the culmination of Kilimanjaro. The air was dainty, and the scene unfurled in the entirety of its stunning greatness. The immense field of the African fields loosened up beneath, and the encompassing pinnacles arose like quiet sentinels in the blurring light.

At that time of tranquility, the hero felt a significant association with the universe. It was the actual rise as well as an otherworldly climb, a converging of the limited self with the endless region. The peak of the story was not a lone occasion but rather a union of the hero's excursion with the inestimable dance of presence.

As the hero looked into the distance, a feeling of disclosure washed over them. It was anything but a booming revelation however a peaceful acknowledgment of insights that had consistently lived inside. The highest point, washed in the delicate tones of sundown, turned into a sacrosanct space where the cloak of deception were lifted, and the substance of oneself was uncovered.

In the quietness of the culmination, the hero heard the murmurs of their own heart. The questions and fears that had went with the excursion were presently supplanted by a significant feeling of clearness. The culmination, however an actual objective, turned into a similitude for the inward levels that can be scaled through boldness, steadiness, and self-disclosure.

The night slipped upon Kilimanjaro, and the stars arose, providing reason to feel ambiguous about their shining light the scene. The hero, presently situated on the highest point, felt a profound feeling of appreciation for the excursion that had carried them to this consecrated space. The story, a long way from arriving at its decision, entered another part - one set apart by the reverberations of the disclosures at the highest point.

In the isolation of the evening, the hero pondered the layers of importance woven into the texture of their excursion. Kilimanjaro, with its transcending presence, turned into an instructor and an aide, offering illustrations that rose above the limits of language and rationale. The peak of the story was not a limited endpoint but rather a start, an entryway to a daily existence lived with reason and credibility.

As the night unfurled, the hero, enclosed by the quiet of the culmination, felt a fellowship with the secrets of presence. The stars above appeared to murmur old stories, and the actual mountain turned into a storehouse of aggregate insight. The culmination, however singular, was a nexus where the singular excursion converged with the all inclusive story.

With the main light of sunrise, the hero plummeted from the highest point, conveying the disclosures scratched into their being. The excursion, presently a drop into the recognizable landscape beneath, held the commitment of a day to day existence changed. The hero, however genuinely lower, felt an inward rise that rose above the pinnacles and valleys of the outer scene.

As the story proceeded, the hero turned into a living demonstration of the disclosures at the culmination. The plunge, set apart by a restored power and a developed grasping, unfurled together as one with the regular rhythms of the mountain. The difficulties looked on the rising currently seemed like venturing stones to a higher plane of presence.

The hero, when a searcher of importance, turned into a guide for others on their own excursions. The disclosures at the culmination were not stored yet shared, a gift proposed to individual voyagers exploring the intricate embroidery of life. The plummet, however a re-visitation of the fields underneath, held the commitment of fresh starts and the constant unfurling of understanding.

In the valleys and levels, in the midst of the dynamic shades of the African scene, the hero experienced individual searchers - close companions attracted to the attractive draw of self-disclosure. The trading of stories and encounters turned into a mutual embroidery, a meshing together of individual strings into an aggregate story.

The disclosures at the highest point, however profoundly private, resounded with a well known fact. The hero, presently an aide and ally to other people, embraced the smoothness of the excursion. Kilimanjaro, when a far off top, turned into an image carved into the shared perspective, a sign of the levels that can be arrived at through mental fortitude and thoughtfulness.

As seasons changed and years passed, the hero saw the recurrent idea of presence. Birth and demise, satisfaction and distress, creation and disintegration - each stage held its own importance in the great ensemble of life. The disclosures, once significant and spectacular, presently appeared in the straightforwardness of regular minutes.

The hero, enhanced with the patina of shrewdness, kept on traveling through the embroidery of presence. Kilimanjaro, however far off in the actual domain, stayed a directing light in the internal scene. The disclosures, similar to a compass, coordinated the hero's way, directing them through the different scenes of life.

In snapshots of tranquility, the hero would shut their eyes and return to the highest point in the openings of their awareness. The murmurs of the mountain winds and the reverberations of the disclosures turned into a wellspring of comfort and motivation. The excursion, a long way from being a direct movement, unfurled as an unending investigation of the endless conceivable outcomes implanted in the embroidery of presence.

In the nightfall of their reality, the hero got back to Kilimanjaro one final time. A truly epic excursion, presently a round trip, conveyed the heaviness of encounters and the lavishness of a spirit that had navigated the profundities of self-revelation. The culmination, washed in the delicate shine of nightfall, invited the fatigued voyager back to where everything started.

As the hero remained on the culmination, a feeling of consummation washed over them. The disclosures, once looked for with intense assurance, had turned into a fundamental piece of their personality. Kilimanjaro, with its quiet grandness, appeared to gesture in affirmation, a quiet observer to the change that had unfurled on its slants.

"Searcher of significance, you have climbed the levels and plumbed the profundities of your own being," murmured the mountain winds. "The highest point was nevertheless a mirror mirroring the insights that live inside. Your process go on past the limits of reality."

With a heart loaded with appreciation, the hero offered a quiet goodbye to Kilimanjaro. The drop, presently a re-visitation of the natural fields beneath, held the commitment of new undertakings. The disclosures, similar to a light helped through the ages, kept on enlightening the way for the people who thought for even a moment to set out on the excursion of self-revelation.

Thus, the story unfurled, not as a single story but rather as a part in the aggregate adventure of searchers who had stepped the way of illumination. Kilimanjaro, however established in the actual domain, turned into an image that rose above the limits of geology. The disclosures at the highest point, similar to an immortal tune, reverberated through the passageways of time, resounding with the enormous rhythms of presence.

The hero, presently a piece of the everlasting dance, blurred into the chronicles of time, abandoning a tradition of boldness, strength, and self-revelation. Kilimanjaro, with its quiet pinnacles, remained as a sentinel, an update that the excursion of the spirit keeps, meshing together the strings of individual stories into the fantastic embroidery of presence. The peak of the story, however focused on the culmination, was not an endpoint but rather an entryway to the boundless conceivable outcomes that anticipated the people who really considered investigating the internal and external scenes of their own being.

7.2 Unveil the long-guarded secrets and the true purpose of Majestic Heights.

In the core of a rambling mountain range, covered in fog and secret, lay Lofty Levels — a spot murmured regarding in quieted tones, hidden in the conundrum of its presence. For ages, the mysteries covered inside the lofty pinnacles had been a wellspring of hypothesis, interest, and wonder. The opportunity had arrived to unwind the long-watched secrets and enlighten the genuine reason that lay secret inside the folds of Lofty Levels.

The excursion to uncover the privileged insights of Glorious Levels started with a solitary explorer, drawn by a strange interest that rose above the limits of customary investigation. The way prompting the levels was not very much trampled; it wandered through thick woods, crossed tempestuous waterways, and rose misleading precipices. The globe-trotter, resolute by the difficulties, went ahead, moved by an internal realizing that the objective held disclosures of significant importance.

As the explorer moved toward Lofty Levels, the air changed. The air became accused of an energy that shivered the skin, and the environmental elements took on an ethereal quality. The pinnacles, covered in unending fog, appeared to entice with a supernatural charm. Maybe the actual mountains held a cognizance that anticipated the appearance of the individuals who tried to disclose the secrets.

At the foundation of Great Levels, the explorer found old vestiges, remainders of a development long neglected. The stones, endured by time, discussed a past period, indicating a once-flourishing local area that had called these levels home. The genuine motivation behind Lofty Levels started to arise, woven into the actual texture of the antiquated stones.

The remnants uncovered mind boggling carvings and images that communicated in a language of images and illustrations. The explorer, with an instinctive comprehension, interpreted the messages scratched into the stones. Glorious Levels, it appeared, was not just a geological area but rather a safe-haven of information, a store of old insight monitored by the actual mountains.

As the swashbuckler dove further into the core of Magnificent Levels, they found a secret chamber hid inside the mountain's rough hug. The entry, decorated with images of divine importance, opened into a cave washed in a delicate, radiant gleam. The air inside reverberated with a murmur that appeared to vibrate with the heartbeat of the actual earth.

In the core of the chamber, the traveler found a gigantic precious stone, throbbing with a brilliant energy that resisted natural clarification. The precious stone, it showed up, was the point of convergence of the insider facts held inside Superb Levels. As the globe-trotter drew nearer, the precious stone answered, projecting pictures and dreams that moved like vaporous dreams.

The dreams uncovered the historical backdrop of Superb Levels, a story that unfurled across ages and civilizations. The mountains had been a safe-haven for searchers of truth, where the limits between the physical and otherworldly domains obscured. The precious stone, mixed with the aggregate insight of the individuals who had preceded, held the keys to opening the secrets that penetrated the levels.

Grand Levels, it was revealed, had filled in as a gathering ground for researchers, spiritualists, and searchers from different societies. The gem, a conductor for vast energies, worked with a fellowship of brains, a sharing of information that rose above phonetic and social hindrances. The mountains, with their innate otherworldly energy, turned into a signal for those attracted to the quest for higher comprehension.

As the swashbuckler drenched themselves in the dreams projected by the gem, they saw social occasions of sages and rationalists, participating in exchanges that rose above the restrictions of natural information. Glorious Levels, it appeared, was an extension between the human and the heavenly, where searchers communed with the inestimable powers that represented the universe.

The reason for Grand Levels, the traveler understood, was to act as a safe-haven for the protection and dispersal of general insights. The gem, going about as an enormous chronicle, put away the insight of ages, protecting it from the ways of the world. The actual mountains, with their remarkable energy signature, had been picked as the overseers of this sacrosanct storehouse.

In the unfurling account, the explorer saw the repetitive idea of civic establishments that had risen and fallen. Lofty Levels had seen the back and forth movement of mankind's set of experiences, and the precious stone had consumed the aggregate encounters, bits of knowledge, and impressions of innumerable ages. It was a living record of the development of cognizance — a demonstration of the interconnectedness of all life.

As the traveler ingested the disclosures, a significant feeling of obligation settled upon them. They comprehended that the information held inside Lofty Levels was not intended to be accumulated however to be imparted to mankind. The precious stone, in its brilliant splendor, appeared to attest this comprehension, throbbing with a power that repeated the criticalness of the mission.

In the core of the mountains, the globe-trotter sincerely promised to convey the insight of Lofty Levels back to the world underneath. The plummet from the levels, however truly descending, felt like a profound climb — a return with a consecrated reason. Superb Levels, when a secret safe-haven, was bound to turn into a guide of enlightenment for the individuals who looked for the more profound bits of insight of presence.

As the globe-trotter slid, they experienced individual searchers who had been attracted to Magnificent Levels by an inconspicuous power. Together, they shaped a local area joined by a common mission for illumination. The disclosures conveyed by the swashbuckler turned into a wellspring of motivation, starting an aggregate arousing that undulated through the texture of the gathering cognizance.

In the valleys and fields underneath Glorious Levels, the traveler and their buddies laid out a middle for learning and otherworldly investigation. The gem, presently painstakingly shipped, turned into the point of convergence of this safe-haven — where searchers from all edges of the world could accumulate and participate in the immortal insight held inside the mountains.

The lessons of Glorious Levels rose above strict creeds and social limits. They addressed the widespread embodiment that joins all of mankind. The precious stone, presently open to those with unadulterated goals, filled in as a course for profound disclosure, offering looks into the interconnected snare of presence.

The safe-haven underneath Great Levels turned into a sanctuary for researchers, thinkers, and spiritualists — where the quest for information was not bound to the scholar however embraced the otherworldly and the supernatural. It turned into a center point for the investigation of cognizance, where the searcher could set out on inward excursions that reflected the rising of the mountains.

As the safe-haven thrived, its impact stretched out a long ways past its actual limits. The lessons of Lofty Levels pervaded into the shared mindset of mankind, igniting a renaissance of profound request and an agreeable mix of different social viewpoints. The precious stone, however genuinely contained, emanated its energy, contacting the hearts and psyches of those receptive to its recurrence.

In the death of seasons and the unfurling of years, the safe-haven underneath Superb Levels turned into a journey site for those looking for a more profound comprehension of oneself and the universe. The precious stone, presently venerated as a hallowed relic, drew pioneers from each side of the globe. The energy of Superb Levels, once restricted to the mountains, presently resounded in the hearts of the people who made the excursion.

The explorer, having satisfied their main goal, kept on dwelling at the safe-haven, imparting the immortal insight to the individuals who looked for direction. The disclosures of Grand Levels, however old, stayed evergreen, adjusting to the advancing cognizance of every age. The gem, as a living vault, kept on beating with the vast energies that had directed the searchers of old.

The safe-haven underneath Grand Levels turned into a demonstration of the extraordinary force of profound investigation. It was anything but a stale foundation however a living organic entity that adjusted to the changing requirements of humankind. The lessons, while established in the ageless, found significance in the contemporary difficulties looked by people and social orders.

As the years passed, the safe-haven turned into an image of solidarity, spanning the partitions that had isolated individuals for a really long time. It filled in as an update that, underneath the surface distinctions, all creatures were interconnected — an acknowledgment that had been carved into the actual stones of Superb Levels. The gem, with its brilliant gleam, turned into a representation for the intrinsic potential for brightening that dwelled inside every person.

In the nightfall of their life, the explorer looked at Glorious Levels from the vantage point of the asylum. The mountains, however far off, appeared to murmur expressions of appreciation, recognizing the pretended by the explorer in uncovering the long-watched mysteries and satisfying the genuine motivation behind the lofty pinnacles.

The globe-trotter, with a heart brimming with satisfaction, passed into the domains past. Their heritage resided on in the safe-haven, where searchers kept on stepping the way of inward investigation. Magnificent Levels, presently a guide of light noticeable to all, remained as a demonstration of the limitless conceivable outcomes that unfurl when the searcher thinks for even a second to uncover the long-protected privileged insights concealed inside the profundities of their own being. The mountains, with their immortal insight, kept on looking after the safe-haven, quietly confirming the interconnectedness of all life and the timeless excursion of self-disclosure.

7.3 Tie together the various elements of the story, providing a satisfying resolution to the mystery.

As the sun plunged beneath the skyline, projecting a warm brilliant gleam upon the scene, the dissimilar strings of the story started to wind around together, meeting toward a peak that guaranteed goal to the well established secret. Glorious Levels, with its old remnants, magical gem, and the safe-haven beneath, remained as the focal point where the perfection of the experience would unfurl.

The hero, having navigated the slippery territory and unwound the puzzling mysteries of Glorious Levels, ended up remaining at the cliff of a significant disclosure. The precious stone, throbbing with brilliant energy, coaxed them toward the core of the safe-haven. The opportunity had arrived to carry intelligence to the pieces of information dissipated across the story.

The safe-haven, a center point for otherworldly investigation and a storehouse of immortal insight, had turned into a social occasion place for searchers from varying backgrounds. The precious stone, presently loved as a holy curio, held the way to interfacing the different components of the story — a vast riddle ready to be settled.

In the delicate shine of the precious stone's luminance, the hero started to cooperative with the energy that reverberated inside. Dreams unfurled, uncovering looks at the past, present, and future. The old destroys, the mountain's enchanted energy, and the combination of different searchers — all assumed a part in the terrific embroidery of Lofty Levels.

The narrative of Superb Levels, it showed up, rose above the constraints of straight time. The remains, with their endured stones, discussed ages a distant memory, while the gem, with its brilliant heartbeat, associated the strings of history to the current second. The safe-haven, with its different local area of searchers, was a living demonstration of the consistently developing nature of the excursion of self-disclosure.

As the hero dove further into the disclosures, a feeling of interconnectedness saturated their cognizance. The old development that once flourished in the shadow of Superb Levels had tried to make a safe-haven where the quest for information, shrewdness, and otherworldly illumination would rise above the limits of time and culture.

The precious stone, implanted with the shared perspective of previous eras, turned into an extension between the ages. It was not simply a lifeless thing but rather a living conductor for the enormous energies that penetrated the universe. The hero, presently receptive to the vibrational recurrence of Lofty Levels, felt a significant obligation to convey forward the disclosures into the world.

The different local area of searchers in the asylum, drawn by an inward calling, had turned into the stewards of Glorious Levels. Researchers, spiritualists, savants, and conventional people looking for significance had figured out something worth agreeing on chasing after higher comprehension. The safe-haven, when an unlikely treasure, had turned into a signal of solidarity in a world frequently divided by contrasts.

The different components of the story — the old destroys, the supernatural gem, the safe-haven, and the local area of searchers — were unpredictably associated, each assuming a part in the disclosure of Great Levels' actual reason. The hero, with recently discovered lucidity, comprehended that the secret was not just about the actual components but rather about the groundbreaking excursion of the human soul.

In the core of the safe-haven, a chamber of savvy people, drawn from the local area of searchers, assembled to observe the unfurling of the climactic goal. The old vestiges, presently seen as images of a neglected progress' journey for information, filled in as a background to the earth shattering event.

The precious stone, transmitting its ethereal gleam, projected pictures that wove together the accounts of people who had once looked for illumination in the shadow of Great Levels.

The hero, a channel for the aggregate insight put away inside the gem, started to portray the stories of the individuals who had preceded, their battles, wins, and the immortal bits of insight they had uncovered.

The safe-haven, reverberating with the amicable vibrations of mutual perspective, turned into a pot of solidarity. The different foundations, societies, and convictions of the searchers converged into an aggregate embroidery that commended the unity of mankind. Grand Levels, it appeared, had forever been an impetus for separating the hindrances that isolated people, welcoming them to perceive the ongoing idea that bound them together.

As the accounts unfurled, the board of shrewd people gestured in affirmation. The secret of Grand Levels, however covered in the fogs of time, was not about a secret fortune or a failed to remember innovation yet about the enduring journey for self-disclosure and the acknowledgment of the interconnectedness of all life.

The hero, with lowliness and veneration, uncovered the disclosures scratched into the gem — the antiquated insight that rose above the impediments of social, worldly, and individual viewpoints. Glorious Levels, a long way from being a simple area, was a condition of cognizance, a consecrated space where searchers from all ages could meet and participate in the grandiose dance of edification.

The people group of searchers, presently illuminated by the disclosures, embraced the obligation gave to them. The safe-haven beneath Great Levels was a position of social event as well as a beacon that transmitted the all inclusive bits of insight revealed by ages of searchers. The precious stone, a vast transmitter, resounded with the aggregate goals of the people who had accumulated in its presence.

As the gathering of savvy people considered the disclosures, a choice was made to impart the insight of Lofty Levels to the world. The safe-haven, when a secret sanctuary, would turn into an open space for every one of the people who looked to leave on the excursion of self-disclosure. The precious stone, with its brilliant sparkle, would go about as an aide, enlightening the way for those with unadulterated expectations.

The hero, presently an overseer of Magnificent Levels' disclosures, assumed the job of an aide and guide. They strolled among the local area of searchers, sharing stories, experiences, and the immortal insight that had been disclosed in the core of the mountains. The different gathering, joined by a typical reason, became representatives of the lessons of Superb Levels, broadening the scope of illumination past the limits of the safe-haven.

The safe-haven, when a position of confinement, presently made its ways for the world. Searchers, drawn by the mysterious air of Superb Levels, ran to the asylum from each edge of the globe. The old remains, when quiet observers to the progression of time, reverberated with the dynamic energy of people participated in the extraordinary excursion of self-revelation.

The hero, directed by the astronomical energies that pervaded Great Levels, went to far off lands, spreading the disclosures like seeds of illumination. The lessons, presently freed from the limits of mystery, resounded with people looking for reason, meaning, and a more profound comprehension of their reality.

As the narratives of Superb Levels spread, the world started to go through an inconspicuous yet significant change. The disclosures, when watched inside the magical mountains, presently undulated through the shared mindset of mankind. The antiquated insight, ageless in its pith, tracked down reverberation with people across societies, religions, and conviction frameworks.

Amidst this worldwide arousing, the hero, presently a senior sage, got back to Magnificent Levels. The mountains, with their timeless loftiness, appeared to invite them back with a quiet knowing. The antiquated remnants, once endured and quiet, presently resounded with the reverberations of stories that had risen above the limits of time.

The gem, throbbing with a peaceful brightness, recognized the hero's excursion and the effect of the disclosures on the world. Lofty Levels, it appeared, had satisfied its motivation — the secret disentangled, the insight shared, and the extraordinary excursion embraced by humankind.

In the end snapshots of the story, the hero, remaining on the natural ground of Great Levels, looked at the skyline with a heart loaded with appreciation. The mountains, when a wellspring of secret and interest, presently remained as observers to the endless capability of the human soul.

As the sun plunged beneath the pinnacles, projecting a last fountain of varieties upon the scene, Lofty Levels stayed a reference point — an image of the continuous excursion of self-revelation and the interconnectedness of all life. The story, however brought to a delightful goal, reverberated in the hearts of the people who had been moved by the disclosures, filling in as an update that the secrets of presence were, fundamentally, an encouragement to investigate the boundless profundities of the internal identity.

Chapter 8

Integration and Transformation

Coordination and change are two essential ideas that penetrate different parts of our reality, from innovation and business to self-awareness and cultural designs. These ideas address the unique cycles through which dissimilar components meet up to make something new and frequently more hearty. Whether in the domain of innovation, where coordination alludes to the consistent interconnection of various frameworks, or in self-improvement, where change means a significant really impact in outlook and conduct, these ideas assume a crucial part in molding our encounters and forming what's to come.

With regards to innovation, incorporation has turned into a foundation of current frameworks and applications. As our dependence on computerized arrangements develops, the requirement for various advances to cooperate proficiently becomes fundamental. Combination, in this sense, is the most common way of associating and planning different frameworks and programming to work as a brought together entirety. This can include connecting data sets, applications, or even whole organizations, permitting them to flawlessly convey and share data. The objective is to upgrade productivity, smooth out processes, and work on generally execution.

In the realm of business, the significance of coordination is amplified. Ventures frequently work with a large number of frameworks — monetary, client relationship the board (CRM), HR, and that's only the tip of the iceberg. Guaranteeing these frameworks convey and work together is fundamental for accomplishing an all encompassing perspective on the association and pursuing informed choices. Endeavor Asset Arranging (ERP) frameworks represent the mix of different business processes into a bound together stage, giving an extensive perspective on tasks, from inventory network the board to monetary following.

As innovation propels, joining stretches out past the limits of individual undertakings. The ascent of interconnected biological systems and the Web of Things (IoT) highlights the requirement for consistent combination on a more extensive scale. Gadgets, sensors, and stages should cooperate amicably to convey the maximum capacity of brilliant urban areas, associated homes, and smart framework. This degree of joining requires normalized conventions, hearty safety efforts, and co-operative endeavors across ventures to make a firm and interoperable mechanical scene.

Be that as it may, reconciliation alone isn't adequate for tending to the intricacies of our quickly advancing world. Change is the corresponding system that achieves significant change, in how things are associated as well as in their actual nature. In the mechanical domain, computerized change has arisen as a trendy expression epitomizing the essential change in organizations' utilization of innovation to drive development, further develop effectiveness, and make new offers.

Computerized change includes reconsidering cycles and utilizing state of the art advances to upgrade the client experience, improve tasks, and encourage development. Distributed computing, man-made reasoning, and information investigation are key empowering influences of computerized change, permitting associations to adjust to changing scenes and gain an upper hand. Besides, computerized change is certainly not a one-time occasion yet a continuous excursion, expecting associations to develop and embrace arising innovations constantly.

The crossing point of coordination and change is especially obvious in the advancement of utilization programming connection points (APIs). APIs act as extensions that empower different programming applications to impart and share information. As innovation develops, APIs become more complex, working with information trade as well as the mix of cutting edge functionalities. APIs are critical in making an establishment for computerized change by permitting organizations to interface with outsider administrations, influence new advances, and adjust to changing business sector elements.

The collaboration among reconciliation and change is likewise reflected in the development of hierarchical designs. Customary progressive models are giving way to additional coordinated and cooperative methodologies, mirroring the requirement for flexibility and advancement.

Cross-utilitarian groups, enabled via consistent correspondence and combination of different ranges of abilities, assume a critical part in driving extraordinary drives. The incorporation of dexterous systems and DevOps rehearses further speeds up the speed of advancement by encouraging joint effort among improvement and tasks groups.

The meaning of incorporation and change stretches out past the domain of innovation and business — it includes self-awareness and cultural change. On an individual level, people frequently go through extraordinary encounters that reshape their points of view and ways of behaving. These changes can be set off by different elements, like instruction, connections, or openness to novel thoughts. Coordination, in this unique circumstance, includes absorbing these extraordinary encounters into one's character, prompting self-awareness and a more nuanced comprehension of the world.

Cultural changes, then again, include the joining of different points of view and the reconsideration of existing standards and designs. Issues like variety, value, and incorporation feature the requirement for cultural change to make more fair and just networks. This requires the combination of various voices and the destroying of foundational boundaries that sustain imbalance. The multifacetedness of coordination and change becomes clear in developments pushing for social change, where various networks meet up to rock the boat and imagine a more comprehensive future.

The areas of brain science and instruction likewise accentuate the interchange among reconciliation and change. Learning, as an extraordinary cycle, includes the coordination of new information and abilities into existing mental designs. Constructivist hypotheses of learning feature the significance of dynamic commitment and the combination of earlier information with new data to work with significant comprehension.

Besides, restorative methodologies frequently revolve around the combination of divided parts of one's mind to encourage recuperating and individual change. The reconciliation of care rehearses, for example, has acquired conspicuousness for of advancing mental prosperity and working with extraordinary encounters. By developing mindfulness and acknowledgment, people can go through significant inside moves that lead to more prominent profound strength and a more agreeable joining of their viewpoints and feelings.

In the domain of biology and ecological supportability, the mix of human exercises with the normal world is vital for encouraging an extraordinary shift towards additional maintainable practices. The idea of regenerative farming, for instance, includes coordinating rural frameworks with biological standards to improve soil wellbeing, biodiversity, and generally speaking environment strength. This reconciliation addresses an extraordinary way to deal with cultivating that goes past regular works on, meaning to reestablish instead of drain normal assets.

Urban areas, as complicated frameworks molded by human exercises, represent the crossing point of coordination and change. Metropolitan arranging that incorporates reasonable practices and embraces creative advancements can change urban areas into more decent, versatile, and harmless to the ecosystem spaces. Shrewd city drives, driven by the joining of information driven advances, intend to upgrade metropolitan proficiency, work on open administrations, and make more associated and responsive networks.

The connection among reconciliation and change is additionally clear in the domain of medical services. The reconciliation of electronic wellbeing records (EHRs) and wellbeing data trade frameworks considers a more durable and complete way to deal with patient consideration. This joining upgrades correspondence among medical services suppliers, prompting further developed analyze, smoothed out therapy plans, and better quiet results. Moreover, the change of medical care conveyance models, for example, the shift towards esteem based care, mirrors a fundamental change pointed toward working on the general nature of medical care administrations.

With regards to worldwide interconnectedness, the mix of different societies, thoughts, and economies has turned into a characterizing component of the contemporary world. Globalization, generally, is a course of incorporating various countries and locales into a more interconnected and reliant framework. This joining has broad ramifications for economies, legislative issues, and social trade. While globalization has added to monetary development and expanded admittance to data, it has additionally raised worries about disparity, social homogenization, and the disintegration of nearby customs.

The extraordinary capability of mix is exemplified in worldwide joint efforts pointed toward tending to worldwide difficulties. Drives like the Unified Countries Supportable Advancement Objectives (SDGs) highlight the requirement for incorporated endeavors to handle issues, for example, destitution, environmental change, and social imbalance. The interconnected idea of these difficulties requires an extraordinary methodology that goes past secluded mediations, requiring nations and associations to cooperate in a coordinated way to make enduring and positive change.

As we explore the intricacies of the 21st hundred years, the mix of different viewpoints and the hug of groundbreaking cycles become fundamental for cultivating flexibility and versatility. The quick speed of mechanical progression, combined with worldwide difficulties, requires a dynamic and incorporated way to deal with critical thinking. Schooling systems should adjust to develop decisive reasoning, innovativeness, and a profound comprehension of the interconnectedness of the world.

8.1 Explore the aftermath of the revelation and how it impacts the protagonist and the community.

The disclosure struck like a thunderclap, an energizing power that undulated through the hero's reality and the closely knit local area that had, up to that point, flourished with a similarity to predictability. The consequential convulsions of this disclosure were not simply bound to the singular mind of the hero yet resounded through the actual texture of the local area, uncovering weaknesses, breaking deceptions, and provoking an aggregate reconsideration of what was once underestimated.

In the consequence, the hero wound up wrestling with a significant feeling of bewilderment. The disclosure, whatever its temperament, had overturned the groundworks of their figuring out, leaving them untied in an ocean of vulnerability. The agreeable accounts that had directed their activities and choices were presently uncovered as delicate develops, dependent upon the impulsive impulses of truth. It was a snapshot of retribution, a showdown with the shadows that hid underneath the outer layer of their reality.

As the hero explored the wild territory of their own feelings, the effect of the disclosure emanated outward, ruining the local area. The shared bonds that had once appeared to be strong now shuddered under the heaviness of newly discovered information. Trust, that fragile string winding through the social texture, started to shred, abandoning a feeling of aggregate weakness. Murmurs of incredulity and selling out reverberated through the local area, and the once-strong ground of mutual perspective appeared to move underneath their feet.

The disclosure, similar to a crevice in the earth, uncovered secret separation points inside the local area elements. Old complaints, covered feelings of hatred, and stifled pressures flooded to the surface, powered by the shock of reality exposed. The people group, when an agreeable embroidery of interconnected lives, presently looked like a mosaic with broke pieces, each mirroring an alternate feature of the aggregate injury. Directly following the disclosure, the local area wound up at a junction, confronted with the decision of either surrendering to the breaks or undertaking the difficult errand of revamping.

For the hero, the consequence of the disclosure appeared as an excursion of self-revelation. The bits of insight they had held dear were presently relics of a past time, and the mission for personality took on another earnestness. The excursion included a difficult uncovering of covered recollections, a returning to of critical minutes from the perspective of this freshly discovered information. Each memory turned into a milestone between what was known and what was currently uncovered, and the hero wrestled with the disrupting errand of accommodating their previous self with the individual exposed by the disclosure.

The close to home scene of the hero reflected the changing times of their inward world. Forswearing, outrage, bartering, gloom — every one of the phases of sadness strutted through their cognizance in a turbulent dance. Every inclination, similar to a brushstroke on the material of their mind, added to the developing representation of an individual in motion. The excursion was not straight; it spiraled and circled, following advances and moving forward, as the hero looked to get a handle on the disturbance inside.

At the same time, the local area went through its very own transformation. The disclosure went about as an impetus for aggregate contemplation, driving the local area individuals to defy awkward insights about themselves and one another. The collective account, when a common story that gave attachment, presently showed up as a delicate develop, defenseless to disentangling. The disclosure had stripped away the facade of aggregate guiltlessness, uncovering the intricacies and logical inconsistencies that stewed underneath the surface.

Even with such disturbance, the local area displayed a range of reactions. Some looked for comfort in fortitude, manufacturing associations with the people who had comparable encounters or points of view. Bonds framed in difficulty turned into a wellspring of solidarity, a help in the midst of the confusion. Others, notwithstanding, withdrew into separation, wrestling with the heaviness of the disclosure in isolation. The common spaces that once cultivated a feeling of having a place presently felt outsider, tormented by the phantom of a reality that had everlastingly changed the scene.

Trust, when an understood underpinning of local area life, presently expected conscious exertion and deliberateness to remake. The delicacy of human connections was exposed, and the local area individuals wound up exploring a fragile dance of weakness and flexibility. Discussions, once held effortlessly, presently tread lightly around the implicit, as people estimated their words against the background of the disclosure. The public quiets said a lot, pregnant with the unsaid inquiries that lingered palpably.

The effect of the disclosure additionally undulated through the shared designs and organizations that had characterized the local area's personality. Laid out ordered progressions and power elements were tested as the disclosure uncovered breaks in the underpinnings of power. The people group, when limited by a common feeling of request, presently wrestled with the tumult of vulnerability. The very instruments intended to keep up with social union presently confronted investigation, and an aggregate renegotiation of standards and values was inescapable.

Inside the microcosm of the local area, collusions moved and realigned because of the disclosure. Groups arose, each upholding for a specific understanding of reality or a favored strategy. The collective talk, when described by a feeling of common perspective, presently turned into a landmark of clashing stories. The hero wound up at the focal point of this philosophical tempest, torn between steadfastness to the past and the basic to embrace a developing future.

The outcome of the disclosure incited a more extensive cultural reflection, reverberating past the bounds of the quick local area. The shapes of the hero's reality stretched out to meet with bigger social designs, and the disclosure accepted more extensive ramifications for the shared perspective. Inquiries of equity, responsibility, and obligation became the overwhelming focus, as the local area wrestled with the moral components of reality revealed.

Chasing equity, the local area went through a course of aggregate retribution. The disclosure went about as an impetus for looking at verifiable treacheries, uncovering foundational disparities, and considering people responsible for their activities. The quest for equity, in any case, was laden with difficulties, as the local area explored the strain between the requirement for responsibility and the basic of compromise. The fragile harmony among retaliation and reclamation turned into an ethical pot, testing the local area's strength and obligation to a common moral system.

The disclosure's effect on the local area's ethical compass stretched out to the domain of administration and social designs. Foundations that had once deserved admiration and authority currently confronted investigation, and calls for change resounded through the shared talk. The people group ended up at an intersection, wrestling with the decision between protecting the state of affairs and embracing groundbreaking change. The heroes, as hesitant pioneers or candid backers, assumed an essential part in molding the local area's reaction to this moral dilemma.

As the hero explored their own odyssey, the local area's reaction to the disclosure turned into a mirror mirroring the more extensive human condition. Subjects of pardoning, recovery, and the chance of recharging penetrated the common account, recommending that even notwithstanding significant commotion, the human soul had a natural limit with regards to flexibility and development. The hero's excursion, interweaved with that of the local area, highlighted the potential for extraordinary change, both at an individual and aggregate level.

The repercussions of the disclosure turned into a cauldron for producing new stories and personalities. The people group, when characterized by a common history, presently remained on the cliff of an aggregate modifying of its story. The hero, as a focal figure in this story development, wrestled with the obligation of molding the local area's future. The inventive strain between saving the extravagance of the past and embracing the vulnerabilities representing things to come turned into a topical inclination, reverberating through the hero's subtle conflicts and the public discussions that unfurled.

Eventually, the outcome of the disclosure turned into a demonstration of the interconnectedness of individual and aggregate predeterminations. The hero's very own excursion of self-disclosure and change repeated the more extensive cultural movements inside the local area.

The disclosure went about as an impetus for a perplexing, complex interaction that incorporated close to home, moral, and underlying aspects. The repercussions was not only an aftermath; it was a pot that fashioned new understandings, tried the constraints of versatility, and laid the preparation for a rethought future.

In the last examination, the fallout of the disclosure turned into a section in the continuous account of the hero's life and the aggregate story of the local area. It was a part set apart by choppiness, reflection, and the potential for reestablishment. The disclosure, with all its troublesome power, turned into an impetus for transformation — an extraordinary second that welcomed both the hero and the local area to stand up to the intricacies of truth, explore the landscape of vulnerability, and, in doing as such, arise on the opposite side with a more profound comprehension of themselves and the world they occupied.

8.2 Highlight personal growth, newfound wisdom, and the integration of the revealed secrets into the lives of the characters.

The disclosure, while seismic and troublesome, filled in as a cauldron for self-awareness among the characters in question. It was an impetus for a significant change, moving them to face awkward insights, reconsider their needs, and leave on an excursion of self-revelation. As the characters wrestled with the aftermath of the disclosure, they wound up exploring unknown profound landscape, each step full of vulnerability however pregnant with the commitment of individual advancement.

For the hero, the excursion of self-awareness unfurled as a progression of contemplative minutes and valiant showdowns with oneself. The disclosure went about as a mirror, reflecting the divulged insider facts as well as the hero's own weaknesses, frailties, and neglected potential. The interaction was likened to a resurrection — a shedding of the old self and a rise of a more true, versatile variant.

The underlying phases of self-awareness were set apart by a significant feeling of confusion. The hero, similar to a boat untethered from its moorings, explored the fierce waters of character and reason. The once natural milestones of their interior scene became clouded, and they wrestled with the agitating idea that the underpinning of their convictions was not so strong as they once suspected. It was a wild period, described by snapshots of uncertainty, disarray, and a crude weakness that uncovered the center of their being.

In the midst of this mayhem, the hero found repositories of solidarity they hadn't perceived previously. The course of self-improvement turned into a trial of versatility, as they faced the inconvenience of vulnerability and inclined toward the uneasiness as opposed to avoiding it. It was a valiant hug of weakness — an affirmation that genuine strength lay not in that frame of mind of dread but rather in the readiness to defy and rise above it.

As the hero dove further into their own mind, they uncovered dormant interests, undiscovered gifts, and a repository of undiscovered possibility. The excursion of self-revelation turned into a festival of genuineness, as they figured out how to embrace the intricacy of their character and coordinate the different features into a durable entirety. The once-covered up corners of their character became wellsprings of solidarity as opposed to disgrace, and the course of self-improvement was set apart by a freshly discovered acknowledgment of both light and shadow.

The disclosure likewise impelled the hero towards a way of recently discovered shrewdness. The insights uncovered, but excruciating, conveyed with them significant examples about existence, connections, and the idea of presence. The most common way of acclimatizing this insight included a profound reflection on the interconnectedness of involvement and the temporariness of sureness. The hero, once fastened to unbending convictions, presently explored the ease of truth with an insightful psyche and an open heart.

Shrewdness, in this unique situation, was not a static state but rather a dynamic, developing comprehension of the world. The hero figured out how to see the value in the subtleties of dim in the midst of the high contrast, perceiving that reality frequently dwelled in the liminal spaces between absolutes. This recently discovered intelligence turned into a directing light, enlightening the way towards a more nuanced, caring commitment with the intricacies of human experience.

The coordination of the uncovered insider facts into the existences of the characters was a groundbreaking interaction, likened to meshing strings of truth into the texture of their reality. It included a sensitive dance among affirmation and greatness, as the characters wrestled with the effect of the disclosure on their connections, viewpoints, and healthy identity.

One part of this incorporation was the recalibration of connections. The disclosure had uncovered the complexities of relational elements, and the characters ended up at a junction — defying the decision among hatred and pardoning, distance and association. The interaction was not straight; it included exploring the back and forth movement of feelings, as characters swayed between snapshots of outrage, sorrow, and, eventually, acknowledgment.

For the hero, the reconciliation of uncovered mysteries into their connections turned into a practice in sympathy and understanding. They perceived the humankind in others, recognizing the imperfections, weaknesses, and secret bits of insight that made every individual remarkable. The once-critical look relaxed into one of empathy, encouraging a more profound association in view of shared mankind as opposed to shallow discernments.

The joining system likewise stretched out to the characters' points of view on themselves. The disclosure had broken deceptions and exposed parts of their character that had extended stayed covered.

This revealing, instead of setting off a plunge into self-hatred, turned into a chance for self-empathy. The characters figured out how to embrace flaw, perceiving that the excursion of self-improvement was a persistent, iterative cycle as opposed to an objective.

In the domain of connections, the coordination of uncovered mysteries ignited an aggregate reexamination of mutual qualities and standards. The people group, when limited by a common story, presently confronted the test of remaking its character following the disclosure. The characters participated in an exchange about the sort of local area they sought to be — manufacturing new arrangements, encouraging inclusivity, and laying out an establishment based on straightforwardness and shared regard.

The joining system likewise elaborate an aggregate retribution with the past. The characters stood up to verifiable treacheries, recognizing the effect of insider facts and implicit bits of insight on the local area's advancement. This retribution turned into a forerunner to a course of aggregate mending, as the characters perceived the need to address the injuries of the past to push ahead. The reconciliation of verifiable insights into the local area's story considered a more extensive comprehension of its aggregate personality and a promise to a more fair future.

As the characters coordinated the uncovered privileged insights into their lives, a feeling of therapy arose — a deep breath of help that went with the unburdening of covered insights. The cycle was not without its difficulties, but rather the characters tracked down strength in weakness, flexibility in transparency, and development in the acknowledgment of awkward insights. The incorporation turned into a demonstration of the groundbreaking force of truth — the capacity to free, recuperate, and establish the groundwork for a more bona fide and interconnected presence.

The coordination of uncovered privileged insights likewise prodded an aggregate obligation to straightforwardness and legitimacy inside the local area. Open correspondence turned into a foundation of collective life, encouraging a climate where people felt enabled to share their bits of insight unafraid of judgment or response. The people group, when cracked by disguised privileged insights, presently blossomed with a culture of receptiveness that reinforced relational bonds and developed a feeling of shared liability regarding the aggregate prosperity.

In the domain of self-improvement, the characters' processes were not without difficulties. The joining of uncovered privileged insights requested strength, as they explored the intricacies of absolution, self-acknowledgment, and the recreation of connections. However, inside this cauldron of difficulties, the characters found an internal guts that impelled them towards freshly discovered levels of the ability to understand people on a profound level and development.

The characters, when bound by the restrictions of their past selves, presently remained at the limit of a more sweeping presence.

The course of self-improvement, powered by the combination of uncovered privileged insights, had catalyzed a transformation — a shedding of old examples, a refinement of character, and a development into a more credible and enabled rendition of themselves.

As the characters embraced this extraordinary excursion, they became signals of motivation inside the local area. Their self-awareness emanated outward, impacting the shared story and catalyzing an aggregate obligation to ceaseless development. The combination of uncovered privileged insights turned into a shared soul changing experience, stamping the difficulties looked as well as the flexibility developed and the insight acquired en route.

Eventually, the outcome of the disclosure, set apart by self-improvement, recently discovered shrewdness, and the mix of uncovered privileged insights, turned into a demonstration of the strength of the human soul. The characters, when restricted by the shadows of hidden insights, presently remained in the brilliant light of legitimacy. The excursion, however challenging, had made ready for a more interconnected, merciful, and mindful presence — a demonstration of the groundbreaking force of truth and the dauntless soul of the individuals who considered leaving on the way of self-revelation and public mending.

8.3 Resolve any lingering conflicts or unanswered questions

The goal of waiting struggles and the enlightenment of unanswered inquiries framed the last venture of this complicated story. As the characters faced the consequence of the disclosure, an embroidery of interconnected storylines unfurled, each string adding to the goal of struggles and the revealing of bits of insight that had remained darkened.

One focal struggle that requested goal was the stressed connections inside the local area. The disclosure had created a shaded area over relational elements, provoking the characters to explore the fragile landscape of pardoning, trust, and compromise. The cycle was neither straight nor basic; it expected a significant eagerness to face the uneasiness of weakness and participate in open, genuine correspondence.

For the hero, settling clashes implied participating in gutsy discussions with those straightforwardly affected by the disclosure. These discoursed turned into a pot for profound recuperating, as the characters faced the torment, selling out, and misconceptions that had rotted following the disclosure. The goal of contentions was not inseparable from deletion; all things considered, it included a common affirmation of the scars passed on by the disclosure and a pledge to recuperating and development.

The people group, as an aggregate substance, wrestled with the test of modifying broke connections. Bunch conversations, worked with by compassion and a common obligation to understanding, became gatherings for collective recuperating. The goal of contentions inside the local area requested a renegotiation of relational elements, encouraging a climate where weakness was met with empathy, and contrasts were embraced instead of disregarded.

The goal cycle likewise required resolving fundamental issues that had added to the contentions inside the local area. The characters perceived that the disclosure had uncovered further cultural designs and power irregular characteristics that should have been destroyed. Drives pointed toward cultivating value, inclusivity, and straightforward administration became necessary to the common goal endeavors. The obligation to resolving fundamental issues was not simply a receptive reaction to the disclosure but rather a proactive step towards building a stronger and just local area.

Unanswered inquiries, such as waiting shadows, requested light. The disclosure had uncovered a horde of privileged insights, however it likewise raised new inquiries about the idea of truth, the intricacies of human connections, and the potential for recovery. The goal interaction included a fastidious disentangling of these inquiries, every disclosure adding a layer of lucidity to the mind boggling story.

The journey for truth turned into a focal subject in the goal of unanswered inquiries. The characters set out on a cooperative excursion to sort out the pieces of the past, filling in the holes left by the disclosure. This interaction included the revelation of privileged insights as well as an aggregate obligation to figuring out the specific situation, inspirations, and results that had formed the characters' activities.

The hero, as the focal figure in this account odyssey, looked for answers for themselves as well as for the more extensive local area. Their mission for truth turned into an extraordinary excursion, one that rose above private increase and dove into the domain of collective comprehension. The goal of unanswered inquiries expected fortitude as well as a readiness to embrace the innate intricacies of human life.

The most common way of settling unanswered inquiries likewise welcomed thoughtfulness and self-disclosure. The characters, constrained by the disclosures, went up against awkward bits of insight about themselves and their parts in the unfurling account. This mindfulness turned into an impetus for self-improvement, as the characters explored the territory of their own weaknesses and arose with a more nuanced comprehension of their own mankind.

The goal of unanswered inquiries likewise elaborate the characters wrestling with the outcomes of their activities. While the disclosure had revealed the secret bits of insight, the characters confronted the test of tolerating liability regarding their parts in the unfurling show. The goal cycle requested responsibility — an affirmation of the effect their decisions had on themselves as well as other people.

Reclamation turned into a strong subject in the goal of unanswered inquiries. The characters, having defied their own defects and recognized the torment they had caused, looked for roads for mending and compromise.

The excursion towards reclamation was not without challenges; it expected genuine endeavors to repair connections, offer to set things right, and, in particular, exhibit a promise to change.

The hero, in their quest for answers and reclamation, turned into an encouraging sign and strength for the local area. Their eagerness to face awkward insights, explore self-awareness, and participate during the time spent mending enlivened others to set out on comparative excursions. The goal of unanswered inquiries turned into a common undertaking — a common obligation to figuring out, empathy, and the chance of groundbreaking change.

As the characters explored the complexities of goal, the account dug into the intricacies of absolution. The disclosure had incurred wounds that ran profound, testing the characters' ability to excuse and be pardoned. The course of pardoning was not a straight direction but rather a dynamic, developing excursion that unfurled over the long run.

For the hero, absolution implied delivering the shackles of disdain and embracing the chance of mending. It included a significant inward shift — a cognizant choice to liberate themselves from the weights of outrage and permit space for development and reestablishment. The goal of contentions inside the local area, hence, became interlaced with the individual and aggregate limit with regards to pardoning.

The people group, as an aggregate substance, confronted the test of developing a culture of pardoning. Bunch conversations, worked with by talented go betweens and local area pioneers, became spaces for recognizing the aggravation caused and communicating authentic regret. The goal cycle included looking for pardoning as well as showing a guarantee to compensation and change.

The goal of struggles and unanswered inquiries likewise provoked a reconsideration of common qualities. The people group, having crossed the cauldron of disclosure, took part in an aggregate discourse about the rules that would direct its future. The characters wrestled with the strain between saving the examples of the past and manufacturing a way towards a more edified, fair future.

The mix of shared values turned into a point of convergence in the goal cycle. The characters perceived that the disclosure had uncovered the weaknesses of existing standards and designs, provoking an aggregate obligation to rethinking a stronger, merciful local area. The goal of contentions and unanswered inquiries became indistinguishable from this more extensive vision of common advancement.

The goal interaction reached out past the relational and cultural domains to incorporate more extensive subjects of equity and compensation.

The characters recognized the need to address verifiable treacheries and foundational awkward nature, perceiving that the disclosure had uncovered further issues that requested review. Drives focused on repayments, value, and underlying changes became fundamental parts of the mutual goal endeavors.

The hero, having explored the intricacies of self-awareness, pardoning, and reclamation, assumed a crucial part in molding the local area's obligation to equity. Their process turned into a directing light for other people, outlining that the goal of struggles and unanswered inquiries required thoughtfulness as well as a proactive position towards redressing foundational issues.

The goal cycle likewise elaborate a fragile dance among conclusion and the acknowledgment of progressing difficulties. The characters, having defied the result of the disclosure, perceived that the excursion of development, pardoning, and equity was a continuous, iterative interaction. The goal of contentions didn't suggest the eradication of scars yet rather a guarantee to mending and remaking, with the comprehension that genuine strength lay in the eagerness to stand up to and rise above difficulties.

As the story arrived at its goal, an embroidery of interconnected stories arose — a demonstration of the characters' ability for development, pardoning, and the aggregate quest for equity. The people group, having navigated the turbulent landscape of disclosure, remained at the limit of a rethought future — one molded by the illustrations gained from the goal of struggles and unanswered inquiries.

In the last examination, the goal cycle turned into a demonstration of the dauntless soul of the characters and the local area. The disclosure, however problematic, catalyzed an extraordinary excursion that unfurled through the complicated interchange of self-awareness, pardoning, and equity. The characters, having faced the shadows of the past, arose not as flawless elements but rather as versatile, developed creatures — produced in the pot of disclosure and joined by a common obligation to making a more humane, fair presence.

In the fallout of the disclosure, the story unfurled with a purposeful beat, winding around together the strings of goal, development, and an aggregate quest for understanding. The characters, having faced the hardship of exposure, wound up at a crossroads that requested both reflection and mutual retribution. The story curve turned into a demonstration of the characters' strength, as they explored the complicated embroidery of post-disclosure presence, tending to clashes and unraveling the bunches of unanswered inquiries.

The goal of struggles arose as a focal subject, requesting the characters to stand up to the cracks that had fissured their connections. The disclosure, similar to a seismic occasion, had shaken the underpinnings of trust, and the characters were entrusted with the burdensome excursion of remaking what had been broken. This cycle was neither quick nor direct, requiring persistence, compassion, and an eagerness to participate in awkward discussions.

For the hero, goal implied facing the shadows that waited right after the disclosure. They left on an excursion of self-reflection, unloading the layers of their own feelings and inspirations. This inside investigation turned into a preface to the outer discourse that looked for them — a gallant showdown of the contentions that had putrefied inside the local area.

The public scene, when set apart by the commonality of shared stories, presently looked like a territory scarred by the disclosure. The goal cycle included an aggregate thoughtfulness, as characters looked to connect the gaps that had opened up in the consequence. Discoursed, at first reluctant and accused of implicit pressures, developed into spaces where complaints were circulated, misconceptions were explained, and the public injuries were recognized.

Trust, a sensitive string that had been frayed by the disclosure, turned into a point of convergence in the goal cycle. Characters wrestled with the test of reconstructing trust, perceiving that it required more than simple words — it requested reliable activities, straightforwardness, and a common obligation to recuperating. The hero, as they continued looking for goal, turned into a guide of weakness, moving others to uncover their own insights and work towards modifying the mutual texture.

The goal of struggles additionally involved addressing the main drivers that had prompted the disclosure. Characters dove into the intricacies of human instinct, inspirations, and the unpredictable dance of decisions that had made way for the divulgence. This cycle was not tied in with relegating fault but rather about understanding the subtleties that had added to the contentions, considering an additional thorough and sympathetic viewpoint.

As the characters explored the landscape of goal, pardoning arose as a crucial subject. The disclosure had left injuries, both profound and crude, and pardoning turned into a balm that might actually recuperate these injuries. The hero, in their excursion of self-improvement, wrestled with the intricacies of pardoning — not as a guileless excusal of the past but rather as a cognizant decision to deliver the hold of hatred and embrace the chance of recharging.

Local area complete pardoning, nonetheless, ended up being a more unpredictable dance. The goal cycle included collective conversations, worked with by gifted middle people, where people explored the scene of regret, compassion, and the earnest quest for recovery. The characters perceived that pardoning was not a one-size-fits-all cycle; it required recognizing the aggravation caused, showing veritable regret, and effectively making progress toward revamping broke connections.

The goal of struggles likewise provoked a reconsideration of collective qualities. The characters perceived that the disclosure had uncovered the weaknesses of existing standards and designs, inciting an aggregate obligation to rethinking a stronger, sympathetic local area. The joining of shared values turned into a point of convergence in the goal cycle.

The characters perceived that the disclosure had uncovered the weaknesses of existing standards and designs, provoking an aggregate obligation to reconsidering a stronger, humane local area. The goal of struggles and unanswered inquiries became indivisible from this more extensive vision of shared development.

All the while, the goal cycle reached out past the relational and cultural domains to include more extensive subjects of equity and compensation. The characters recognized the need to address verifiable shameful acts and fundamental irregular characteristics, perceiving that the disclosure had uncovered further issues that requested change. Drives focused on repayments, value, and underlying changes became fundamental parts of the public goal endeavors.

As the account unfurled, unanswered inquiries cast shadows over the's comprehension characters might interpret their reality. The disclosure had gone about as a vital that opened secret offices of truth, however it likewise raised new requests, welcoming the characters to dig further into the intricacies of human life.

The journey for truth turned into a focal subject in the goal of unanswered inquiries. The characters set out on a cooperative excursion to sort out the sections of the past, filling in the holes left by the disclosure. This interaction included the revelation of insider facts as well as an aggregate obligation to grasping the specific situation, inspirations, and results that had formed the characters' activities.

The hero, as the focal figure in this account odyssey, looked for answers for themselves as well as for the more extensive local area. Their mission for truth turned into a groundbreaking excursion, one that rose above private increase and dug into the domain of collective comprehension. The goal of unanswered inquiries expected mental fortitude as well as an eagerness to embrace the inborn intricacies of human life.

The most common way of settling unanswered inquiries additionally welcomed thoughtfulness and self-revelation. The characters, constrained by the disclosures, went up against awkward insights about themselves and their parts in the unfurling story. This mindfulness turned into an impetus for self-improvement, as the characters explored the territory of their own weaknesses and arose with a more nuanced comprehension of their own humankind.

The goal of unanswered inquiries likewise elaborate the characters wrestling with the results of their activities. While the disclosure had exposed the secret insights, the characters confronted the test of tolerating liability regarding their parts in the unfurling show. The goal cycle requested responsibility — an affirmation of the effect their decisions had on themselves as well as other people.

Reclamation turned into an impactful topic in the goal of unanswered inquiries. The characters, having faced their own blemishes and recognized the agony they had caused, looked for roads for recuperating and compromise. The excursion towards reclamation was not without any trace of difficulties; it expected earnest endeavors to patch connections, offer to set things right, and, in particular, show a guarantee to change.

The hero, in their quest for answers and reclamation, turned into an encouraging sign and versatility for the local area. Their process turned into a directing light, showing that the goal of struggles and unanswered inquiries required thoughtfulness as well as a proactive position towards correcting foundational issues.

The goal interaction likewise elaborate a sensitive dance among conclusion and the acknowledgment of continuous difficulties. The characters, having defied the consequence of the disclosure, perceived that the excursion of development, pardoning, and equity was a continuous, iterative cycle. The goal of struggles didn't suggest the eradication of scars yet rather a pledge to mending and remaking, with the comprehension that genuine strength lay in the readiness to stand up to and rise above difficulties.

As the story arrived at its goal, an embroidery of interconnected stories arose — a demonstration of the characters' ability for development, pardoning, and the aggregate quest for equity. The people group, having navigated the wild territory of disclosure, remained at the edge of a reconsidered future — one formed by the illustrations gained from the goal of contentions and unanswered inquiries.

In the last examination, the goal cycle turned into a demonstration of the unyielding soul of the characters and the local area. The disclosure, however problematic, catalyzed a groundbreaking excursion that unfurled through the unpredictable exchange of self-improvement, pardoning, and equity. The characters, having defied the shadows of the past, arose not as perfect elements but rather as strong, developed creatures — produced in the pot of disclosure and joined by a common obligation to making a more humane, fair presence.

Chapter 9

Reflection and Legacy

In the embroidery of human life, woven with strings of encounters, goals, and connections, there exists a significant requirement for reflection. It is in the peaceful snapshots of thought that people navigate the hallways of their recollections, looking for importance and figuring out in the complicated examples of their lives. Reflection is an immortal pursuit, a contemplative excursion that traverses societies, ages, and ages. As the sun sets on one's life, the shadows cast by the decisions, accomplishments, and disappointments make a mosaic that characterizes one's inheritance.

At the core of reflection lies the ability to address, to test the profundities of one's spirit and get a handle on the horde occasions that shape the story that could only be described as epic. An interaction rises above the commonplace, welcoming people to defy their weaknesses, commend their victories, and accommodate with their second thoughts. This thoughtfulness isn't bound to snapshots of emergency or isolation; rather, a continuous discourse with oneself unfurls in the standard embroidery of everyday presence.

In the maze of memory, memories arise as parts of an immense mosaic, each piece adding to the development of individual personality. These parts are not static; they advance with the progression of time, getting new layers of importance and importance. A youth venture might change into a basic example, and an energetic sentiment might develop into a wellspring of getting through intelligence. From the perspective of reflection, the story of one's life turns into a no nonsense element, open to reevaluation and rediscovery.

Heritage, frequently viewed as the effect had on the ways of the world, is an expansion of this intelligent cycle. It is the reverberation of a daily routine very much experienced, reverberating through the hallways of history and molding the shared perspective of people in the future. While the term inheritance might inspire pictures of glory and perpetual quality, it isn't bound to the domains of distinction or fortune. At its center, heritage is the engraving left on the hearts and brains of others — a demonstration of the qualities, standards, and interests that characterized a singular's excursion.

Chasing after understanding one's inheritance, it is fundamental to perceive the unique transaction between the individual and the public. A heritage isn't fashioned in disengagement; it is a cooperative creation, impacted by the connections, networks, and social orders in which an individual is implanted. The reverberations of an inheritance resonate through familial bonds, companionships, and the more extensive embroidery of human association. In this interconnected dance, people track down both the material and the brush to paint the strokes of their effect on the world.

As reflections entwine with heritages, a cooperative relationship arises — one impacting the other in a constant criticism circle. The intelligent look enlightens the way voyaged, offering experiences into the inspirations that impelled activities and the examples advanced en route. All the while, the heritage cast by one's decisions turns into a mirror, reflecting back the results of those choices and the waves they make in the stream of time.

The heritage isn't bound to unmistakable ancient rarities or landmarks. It reaches out into the immaterial domains of impact, motivation, and change. The educator who grants information, the craftsman who catches the pith of the human experience, the pioneer who controls a local area toward progress — all add to the huge embroidery of inheritances that shape the story of mankind. In this sweeping scene, every person, regardless of cultural height, assumes a part in the aggregate tradition of the human story.

However, the entwining of reflection and inheritance isn't without its intricacies. As people wrestle with the shadows of their past, they go up against the certainty of defect. Slip-ups, laments, and unfulfilled desires cast their own examples in the mosaic of reflection. It is in recognizing these blemishes that the genuine profundity of reflection arises — a readiness to face weakness, gain from disappointments, and outline a course of development and strength.

The intelligent excursion is certainly not a straight direction however a wandering odyssey set apart by pinnacles of delight and valleys of distress. In these vacillations, people track down the natural substance for their heritage — the credibility of lived insight. The heritage, a long way from a perfect scene, is a story enhanced by the tints of misfortune, the nuances of empathy, and the versatility produced in the cauldron of difficulties.

In the domain of reflection, the idea of time takes on a smoothness that rises above customary estimations. It isn't restricted to the ticking of seconds, minutes, and hours yet ventures into the sweeping material of memory and expectation. The past is certainly not a static element; it is a living chronicle, dependent upon reevaluation and the particular focal point of memory. The future, a material yet to be painted, entices with the commitment of conceivable outcomes and the vulnerability of the unexplored world.

The exchange of reflection and heritage stretches out past the individual, reverberating in the shared awareness of social orders and civilizations. History, as the narrative of human undertakings, is a demonstration of the getting through exchange among at various times. It is through the intelligent focal point that social orders wrestle with the intricacies of their stories, recognizing wins and standing up to the shadows of treacheries. The heritage, thusly, turns into a directing power — a compass that focuses toward the beliefs and values considered deserving of safeguarding and progression.

In the mosaic of cultural reflection, the accounts of minimized voices come to the front, testing winning standards and reshaping the shapes of aggregate memory. As social orders wrestle with the traditions of expansionism, fundamental persecution, and social deletion, the intelligent look turns into a device for destroying settled in stories and fashioning a more comprehensive and evenhanded heritage. The acknowledgment of different viewpoints and the enhancement of quieted voices reclassify the actual texture of cultural memory.

At the junction of individual and aggregate reflection lies the significant obligation to develop a heritage that rises above the limits of personal responsibility. The decisions made by people swell outward, affecting the embroidery of networks, countries, and the worldwide human family. In a period set apart by interconnectedness, the effect of individual activities reaches out a long ways past geographic lines, highlighting the earnestness of an aggregate reflection on the heritage humankind is making for people in the future.

The mechanical scene of the current period acquaints new aspects with the intelligent interaction and reshapes the shapes of heritage. The computerized impressions left by people in the virtual domain become a permanent piece of their heritage, making a perplexing exchange between the simple and the computerized. Virtual entertainment stages, websites, and online gatherings act as cutting edge chronicles, catching the contemplations, goals, and connections that characterize contemporary presence.

The computerized age, with its extraordinary admittance to data and worldwide network, presents the two potential open doors and difficulties in forming heritages. On one hand, it offers a stage for people to intensify their voices, share their accounts, and interface with a worldwide crowd. Then again, the computerized domain amplifies the outcomes of activities, making the intelligent interaction a public undertaking subject to examination and understanding. The perpetual quality of computerized antiquities brings up issues about the pliability of personality and the expected mutilation of heritages in the period of data.

In the unpredictable dance of reflection and heritage, the idea of initiative arises as a directing power. Pioneers, whether in the domains of governmental issues, business, or local area, bear the heaviness of forming their own heritage as well as the tradition of the substances they steward. Administration, in its quintessence, is a nonstop demonstration of reflection — a powerful commitment with the intricacies of navigation, vision-setting, and the effect of one's activities on the aggregate story.

Powerful initiative rises above the nearsightedness of transient increases, embracing a comprehensive view that thinks about the drawn out results of choices. The tradition of a pioneer is unpredictably woven into the texture of the associations, establishments, or developments they lead. It is a demonstration of their capacity to explore vulnerability, motivate others, and leave an enduring engraving on the scenes they possess.

As pioneers wrestle with the difficulties of the contemporary world, the basic for moral reflection becomes central. The tradition of pioneers isn't exclusively estimated by monetary achievement or political ability; it is similarly characterized by the moral underpinnings of their decisions. The intelligent pioneer participates in a persistent discourse with their qualities, questioning the moral elements of their choices and the ramifications for the prosperity of the networks they serve.

In the fabulous embroidery of human life, artistic expressions arise as an unmistakable string — an imaginative articulation that rises above the limits of language and culture. Through writing, music, visual expressions, and performing expressions, people channel the intricacies of their intelligent excursions into suggestive structures that resound across reality. The tradition of creative articulation is a demonstration of the force of the human soul to rise above the commonplace and contact the brilliant.

Specialists, as stewards of feeling and creative mind, make heritages that persevere as ageless signals of human innovativeness. The strokes of a painter's brush, the rhythm of a performer's tune, and the expressiveness of an essayist's composition become deified in the aggregate memory of humankind. Human expression, in their heap structures, become a mirror mirroring the goals, battles, and wins of civic establishments — a heritage that rises above the ephemerality of individual lives.

In the mission for a significant heritage, the idea of direction arises as a directing star. Object is certainly not a static objective however a unique power that moves people forward, mixing their activities with goal and importance. The intelligent excursion is, basically, a journey for reason — a ceaseless investigation of the qualities and rules that loan profundity and importance to one's presence.

The tradition of direction is complicatedly attached to the effect people have on the prosperity of others and the more extensive world. The acknowledgment of interconnectedness urges people to consider the moral elements of their interests and the far reaching influence of their decisions on the embroidered artwork of human experience. In a world wrestling with squeezing difficulties, from natural emergencies to social disparities, the tradition of direction turns into a compass directing people toward aggregate prosperity.

Schooling, as the pot where brains are molded and points of view are framed, assumes a vital part in the intelligent cycle and the development of heritage. The study hall turns into a space for the investigation of thoughts, the showdown of different perspectives, and the supporting of decisive reasoning abilities. Teachers, as draftsmen of scholarly scenes, employ huge impact in forming the intelligent limits of the future.

The tradition of training reaches out past the transmission of information to the development of values, sympathy, and a feeling of metro obligation. In a period portrayed by quick mechanical progressions and data over-burden, the intelligent abilities developed in instructive settings become fundamental apparatuses for exploring intricacy and adding to the advancement of society. The tradition of training, in this manner, turns into a reference point of edification, directing people toward a more educated and humane presence.

In the dance of reflection and heritage, the idea of versatility arises as a repetitive theme. Versatility isn't simply the capacity to get through difficulties yet a powerful course of variation, learning, and development despite misfortune. The intelligent individual draws upon the wellspring of versatility to stand up to mishaps, gain from disappointments, and arise more grounded from the pot of life's preliminaries.

The tradition of versatility stretches out past individual accounts to envelop the aggregate soul of networks and countries. Despite worldwide difficulties, from pandemics to international strains, flexibility turns into an aggregate undertaking — a common obligation to enduring tempests, supporting each other, and building an additional reasonable and evenhanded future. The tradition of versatility, manufactured in the cauldron of difficulties, turns into a demonstration of the dauntless soul of the human family.

At the convergence of reflection and heritage, the idea of mortality creates its shaded area — a sign of the limited idea of human life. The consciousness of mortality injects the intelligent excursion with a need to get a move on, provoking people to defy the fundamental inquiries of significance and reason.

The heritage, thusly, turns into an extension between the worldly and the everlasting — a method for rising above the limits of individual life expectancies and add to the continuous story of humankind.

The ceremonies of recognition, from memorial services to commemorations, act as strong articulations of the interaction among reflection and inheritance. At these times, networks assemble to respect the existences of the people who have passed, pondering their commitments, the examples gained from their excursions, and the persevering through influence they abandon. The heritage, in the domain of recognition, turns into a wellspring of comfort and motivation — an update that even despite mortality, people can shape stories that outlast their natural presence.

In the excellent woven artwork of human life, the quest for reflection and heritage rises above social, strict, and philosophical limits. A general journey traverses the ages, resounding in the insight of old sages, the creative articulations of different societies, and the moral lessons of otherworldly customs. The acknowledgment of shared mankind turns into a bringing together string, winding around together the horde reflections and heritages that characterize the mosaic of human development.

As the account of reflection and inheritance unfurls, it becomes clear that the mission for importance is a getting through part of the human condition. Whether through logical request, creative articulation, philosophical thought, or otherworldly investigation, people try to get a handle on their reality and add to a story that stretches out past the bounds of individual lives. In this aggregate pursuit, the intelligent excursion and the development of heritage become strings in the rich embroidery of the human story.

All in all, the dance of reflection and heritage is an immortal investigation, a mind boggling movement that shapes the story of individual lives and the shared perspective of mankind. It is an excursion set apart by the rhythmic movement of encounters, the interchange of decisions and outcomes, and the nonstop mission for significance and reason. As people look into the intelligent pool of their lives, they cast swells that resound through the immense scope of human life, abandoning an inheritance that turns into a necessary piece of the continuous story of the human story.

9.1 Conclude the story with reflections on the journey and the significance of the secrets uncovered.

As the sun plunged beneath the skyline, projecting a warm gleam over the scene, I ended up remaining at the junction of an excursion that had unfurled surprisingly. The way I had track, loaded down with exciting bends in the road, had driven me to the core of mysteries long covered, and the heaviness of those disclosures hung weighty in the air. The excursion, similar to an embroidery woven with strings of secret and revelation, had brought me into its complex examples, each step uncovering layers of truth and duplicity.

The story started harmlessly, an opportunity experience with an old diary in the dusty files of a failed to remember library. The blurred pages discussed a former time, of lives weaved in a snare of mystery and interest. The characters, long consigned to the neglected corners of history, murmured through the yellowed material, coaxing me to unwind the puzzle that bound their destinies.

As the story unfurled, I wound up brought into the existences of the people who had strolled similar earth hundreds of years prior. Their delights and distresses, wins and misfortunes, were revealed before me. The mysteries, painstakingly monitored by the progression of time, arose like phantoms from the shadows, tormenting the present with the reverberations of a past that wouldn't be quieted.

The meaning of the mysteries revealed lay not only in that frame of mind of long-covered realities however in the brightening of the human condition. It became obvious that insider facts, similar to shadows, cast their impact over the direction of lives, forming fates and leaving permanent engravings on the texture of presence. The force of these mysteries lived in the actual realities as well as in the feelings, thought processes, and results that hid underneath the surface.

In the faint light of the chronicles, I sorted out a story of affection and selling out, of desires obstructed and dreams broke. The characters, once restricted to the openings of failed to remember history, tracked down a voice through the pages of the diary. Their accounts, however set against the scenery of an alternate period, reverberated with all inclusive topics — love, misfortune, desire, and the lasting journey for importance.

As the account unfurled, I turned into an accidental accessory in the uncovering of covered insights. The excursion turned into a mirror, reflecting not just the existences of those I tried to see yet additionally my own weaknesses, predispositions, and biases. The demonstration of revealing privileged insights was not a confined investigation but rather an instinctive commitment with the intricacies of the human experience.

The excursion, similar to a stream moving through time, brought me through scenes both recognizable and outsider. It turned into a demonstration of the interconnectedness of human stories, the strings of one story meshing consistently into the embroidery of another. The mysteries, when disconnected parts, converged into a durable story that rose above individual lives, resounding in the aggregate memory of a local area and, likewise, the more extensive human family.

The meaning of the mysteries lay in the narratives they told as well as in the inquiries they presented. In the transaction of disclosure and uncertainty, I faced the restrictions of assurance and the ease of authentic stories.

The privileged insights, instead of giving conclusive responses, became impetuses for a more profound investigation into the idea of truth, memory, and the development of verifiable stories.

As I dug further into the maze of the past, I wrestled with the moral components of revealing mysteries that had for some time been dispatched to obscurity. The heaviness of obligation hung weighty on my shoulders, an acknowledgment that the demonstration of removal conveyed ramifications for the relatives of those whose accounts I tried to revive. The meaning of the mysteries stretched out past simple verifiable interest; it conveyed suggestions for the living, opening injuries that had been fixed with the progression of time.

The mysteries, it appeared, were not inactive elements ready to be found; they were living powers with the possibility to shape the present. decisions chasing truth reverberated past the files, impacting the accounts of those associated with the tales I looked to uncover. It was a fragile dance between the obligation to enlighten the shadows of the past and the obligation to explore the moral intricacies of narrating.

In the maze of disclosure, I tracked down comfort in the force of compassion. The mysteries, when covered in the fogs of time, became gateways into the hearts and psyches of the people who had strolled the earth before me. The demonstration of uncovering their accounts turned into a practice in sympathy, an acknowledgment that the intricacies of the human experience rose above the limits of time and culture. The meaning of the mysteries lay in the realities they uncovered as well as in the ability to connect the transient hole and associate with the feelings and goals of people a distant memory.

The excursion, as it approached its decision, incited reflections on the idea of verifiable request and the job of the narrator. The privileged insights uncovered were not static ancient rarities to be indexed and filed; they were living accounts requesting understanding and contextualization. The narrator, in meshing the strings of the past into a lucid story, turned into an overseer of importance, entrusted with the obligation of regarding the subtleties and intricacies of human experience.

The meaning of the privileged insights, it turned out to be clear, stretched out past the bounds of individual stories to the more extensive comprehension of history as a dynamic, developing embroidery. The demonstration of revealing privileged insights was not a straight walk toward a conclusive endpoint but rather a repeating interaction of disclosure, reflection, and reevaluation. The past, a long way from being a stale store of realities, was a living element with the ability to shape contemporary viewpoints and impact the directions representing things to come.

As I remained at the junction, the heaviness of the mysteries rested not as a weight but rather as a gift — an encouragement to draw in with the wealth and intricacy of the human story. The excursion had been a demonstration of the flexibility of stories, their ability to persevere through the ages and reverberate with the hearts of those able to tune in.

The meaning of the mysteries lay in their capacity to rise above the limits of existence, becoming extensions that associated unique ages and people.

In the last sections of the excursion, I wrestled with the certainty of deficiency. The insider facts, similar to sections of a mosaic, indicated a bigger picture that stayed subtle. The holes in the story, the quiets that reverberated through the chronicles, were tokens of the inborn constraints of authentic request. The meaning of the insider facts, it appeared, lay in what was uncovered as well as in the acknowledgment of the secrets that endured, welcoming people in the future to proceed with the mission for understanding.

The reflections on the excursion reached out past the limits of authentic request to include more extensive subjects of personality, memory, and the human condition. The mysteries, as vessels of memory, conveyed the reverberations of lives that had molded the shapes of a local area and, likewise, the aggregate character of mankind. The demonstration of uncovering these privileged insights turned into a token of reverence to the individuals who had preceded, an acknowledgment that their accounts were necessary to the unfurling story of mankind's set of experiences.

In the sundown of the story, I wound up remaining at the combination of over a wide span of time, an observer to the transaction of stories that rose above individual lives. The mysteries, when secret in the openings of time, had become strings woven into the texture of a bigger embroidery — a demonstration of the interconnectedness of human encounters. The meaning of the mysteries lay in the subtleties they uncovered as well as in the greeting they reached out to draw in with the intricacy and variety of the human story.

The excursion, with its disclosures and reflections, turned into a representation for the more extensive human mission for understanding and importance. The mysteries, however established in a particular verifiable setting, reverberated with immortal topics that navigated ages and societies. The meaning of the mysteries lay in their capacity to act

| 193 |

as mirrors, mirroring the widespread parts of the human condition and welcoming consideration on the common strings that tight spot mankind together.

As I finished up the story, the reverberations of the mysteries waited in the air, an update that the excursion was not a lone pursuit but rather an aggregate undertaking traversing ages. The meaning of the mysteries, it appeared, lay in their uncovering as well as in the continuous exchange they encouraged — a discussion among over a significant time span, between the narrator and the crowd, and between the known and the mysterious.

In the last snapshots of the story, I remained at the limit of a fresh start, conveying with me the heaviness of stories that had risen above the limits of time. The mysteries, when hidden in haziness, had become reference points enlightening the way ahead — a way that welcomed further investigation, request, and reflection.

The meaning of the mysteries, similar to a light passed starting with one age then onto the next, lay in their ability to ignite the flares of interest and figuring out in the hearts of those yet to set out on their own excursions of revelation.

In the embroidery of the human story, the mysteries uncovered were nevertheless a section — a part of a bigger story that kept on unfurling. The meaning of the mysteries, it turned out to be clear, lay not in their conclusion but rather in their job as impetuses for a ceaseless excursion of investigation and translation. The mysteries, when held hostage by the progression of time, had become seeds established in the rich soil of human interest, bound to grow into new stories and appearance in the consistently advancing adventure of mankind.

9.2 Consider the legacy left behind by the protagonist and the impact on Majestic Heights.

In the peaceful town of Grand Levels, where time appeared to move at a deliberate speed and the reverberations of the past resounded through the cobblestone roads, a hero arose whose heritage would draw itself into the actual texture of the local area. This unpretentious figure, with a heart on fire with dreams and a soul unfaltering notwithstanding challenges, left on an excursion that would rise above private desires and make a permanent imprint on Great Levels.

The story of the hero's life unfurled against the background of a town that, while enchanting and saturated with custom, held onto its portion of battles and undiscovered capacity. Grand Levels, with its noteworthy design and affectionate local area, demonstrated the veracity of the rhythmic movement of time, and the hero, in their quest for something more prominent, turned into an impetus for change.

At the center of the inheritance abandoned by the hero was a steady quest for local area government assistance. The hero, perceiving the idle likely inside Great Levels, imagined a future where the town could flourish financially, socially, and socially. This vision was not a far off deliberation but rather a substantial power that moved the hero to activity, drawing in with the local area to plant the seeds of progress.

Financial rejuvenation turned into a foundation of the hero's inheritance. Grand Levels, when described by interesting appeal however wrestling with monetary stagnation, saw a change energized by the hero's enterprising soul. Private ventures thrived, high quality undertakings tracked down a stage, and the once-torpid town square turned into an energetic commercial center, clamoring with movement and life. The tradition of financial strengthening left by the hero was not just a mathematical development in income but rather a resurgence of local area pride and independence.

The effect of the hero's endeavors undulated through the social texture of Magnificent Levels. Local area securities fortified as inhabitants, motivated by the hero's model, worked together on drives that praised variety and inclusivity.

Social celebrations, local meetings, and shared spaces became roads for manufacturing associations and encouraging a feeling of having a place. The tradition of social attachment passed on by the hero was a demonstration of the groundbreaking force of solidarity in a town where everybody knew one another's name.

Training, as well, arose as a point of convergence of the hero's inheritance. Perceiving the significance of information as an impetus for individual and aggregate development, the hero supported drives to upgrade instructive open doors in Superb Levels. Schools thrived, libraries extended, and grant programs opened entryways for trying personalities. The tradition of instructive strengthening passed on by the hero was a pledge to sustaining the scholarly capital of Magnificent Levels, guaranteeing that people in the future would acquire a town wealthy in learning and development.

Natural stewardship turned into an essential piece of the hero's inheritance, as Superb Levels embraced reasonable practices and green drives. Parks prospered, local area gardens sprouted, and the once-contaminated riverbanks went through rebuilding. The tradition of ecological cognizance passed on by the hero was a guarantee to saving the regular magnificence of Glorious Levels, guaranteeing that the town would stay a shelter for a long time into the future.

In the domain of human expression, the hero's heritage was a festival of imagination and articulation. Grand Levels, when eclipsed by its more cosmopolitan neighbors, turned into a social center point, drawing in craftsmen, artists, and entertainers from all over. The tradition of creative liveliness left by the hero was not only the decoration of the town with paintings and figures however an encouraging of a climate where creative mind could flourish, and the human soul could take off.

The hero's very own process became entwined with the account of Grand Levels, and the heritage left behind was an assortment of achievements as well as an account of flexibility, assurance, and the unfaltering confidence in the capability of a local area. The hero's effect on Superb Levels was not a simple succession of occasions but rather an extraordinary excursion that revived the town's actual soul.

The meaning of the hero's inheritance stretched out past the actual changes of Lofty Levels; it ventured into the hearts and brains of the occupants who, propelled by the hero's model, turned into the stewards of their own predeterminations. The heritage was a flash that lighted the flares of plausibility, enabling people to dream, yearn for, and to add to the continuous story of Superb Levels.

In the sundown of the hero's life, as the town luxuriated in the sparkle of its newly discovered imperativeness, reflections on the excursion uncovered the profundity of the effect. Magnificent Levels had become in excess of a background; it had turned into a living demonstration of the

hero's vision and the aggregate desires of its occupants. The inheritance left behind was not a static artifact but rather a powerful power, encouraging the town to keep developing, adjusting, and embracing the soul of progress.

The hero's story became woven into the oral custom of Great Levels, went down through ages as a wellspring of motivation. The heritage, a long way from being ancient history, stayed alive in the narratives told by guardians to their youngsters, in the clamoring markets that demonstrated the veracity of monetary resurgence, and in the giggling that reverberated through local meetings. Lofty Levels, once in danger of blurring into haziness, had turned into a reference point of versatility and restoration — a demonstration of the extraordinary force of one person's vision.

The meaning of the mysteries revealed in the hero's process lay not in outrageous disclosures or secret plans but rather in the widespread insights they enlightened. The insider facts were the strings that wove together the embroidery of the human experience — the battles, the victories, the snapshots of weakness, and the aggregate strength of a local area. They highlighted the hero's humankind, depicting a figure who, notwithstanding their effect, wrestled with vulnerabilities, confronted misfortune, and explored the intricacies of individual and mutual development.

As the local area considered the mysteries revealed in the hero's excursion, an aggregate comprehension arose — an acknowledgment that the human experience, with every one of its complexities, was a common embroidery. The mysteries turned into a mirror, welcoming people to face their own weaknesses, recognize the subtleties of their accounts, and figure out something worth agreeing on in the widespread excursion of self-revelation and local area improvement.

The effect of the hero's inheritance on Superb Levels was not restricted to the substantial results of financial development, social attachment, and ecological maintainability. It resounded in the immaterial domains of motivation, trust, and the conviction that positive change was conceivable as well as reachable through aggregate exertion. The inheritance was an update that each person, no matter what their experience or situation, held the ability to shape the story of their local area and add to a heritage that rose above private desires.

In the last reflections on the excursion, the hero's heritage remained as a demonstration of the groundbreaking expected implanted in the human soul. Great Levels, when a town trapped in the hold of stagnation, had turned into a living demonstration of the hero's conviction that the aggregate activities of a local area could rethink its predetermination. The inheritance left behind was not an end but rather a greeting — a call to people in the future to proceed with the story, to uncover their own mysteries, and to expand upon the establishment laid by the individuals who preceded.

As the sun set over Magnificent Levels, creating long shaded areas that moved across the revived town square, the reverberations of the hero's heritage waited in the air. The excursion, with every one of its preliminaries and wins, had turned into a section in the continuous story of human flexibility and collective development. Grand Levels, when a scenery to the hero's yearnings, had turned into a living demonstration of the persevering through effect of a solitary person's vision and the aggregate strength of a local area joined in reason.

9.3 End with a sense of closure and the promise of new beginnings for the characters and the region.

As the sun plunged beneath the skyline, projecting a warm and brilliant gleam over the rambling scene, the characters in this complex story ended up at the junction of conclusion and fresh starts. The story, woven with strings of intricacy, development, and interconnected fates, arrived at a purpose in climax, abandoning an embroidery rich with encounters, changes, and the commitment of prospects yet to unfurl.

The focal characters, each having navigated a particular bend of improvement, remained on the slope of their own excursions. Their singular stories, laced by destiny and decision, had confounded in manners unexpected, making a mosaic of shared encounters that painted the material of their aggregate presence. As the last sections unfurled, a feeling of conclusion penetrated the air, offering a second for reflection on the preliminaries confronted, the examples learned, and the flexibility found in the cauldron of difficulties.

In the domain of self-improvement and self-disclosure, the characters arose as transformed adaptations of their previous selves. The hero, once unsure and reluctant, had tracked down the solidarity to defy inward evil presences and embrace realness. The excursion of self-disclosure, set apart by thoughtfulness and snapshots of weakness, had prompted a significant comprehension of personality and reason. As the hero looked into the figurative mirror, the reflection was one of newly discovered certainty, a demonstration of the flexibility of the human soul notwithstanding difficulty.

Going with the hero on this excursion was a cast of supporting characters, each adding to the embroidery of development and change. Companions became mainstays of help, tutors gave direction, and foes, once saw as snags, uncovered themselves as impetuses for change. The conclusion of their singular circular segments was not just the tying of last details but rather a festival of the complicated dance of connections and the effect they had on molding the characters' fates.

The topics of affection and association, entwined with the intricacies of human connections, arrived at a crescendo in the last ventures. Heartfelt snares, when wellsprings of contention and disarray, tracked down goal in the woven artwork of understanding and shared development.

The connections that endured the everyday hardships and adversity arose more grounded, their bonds developed by shared encounters and a common obligation to exploring the intricacies of adoration.

Family, as well, assumed a crucial part in the story conclusion. Compromises, absolution, and the mending of wounds shaped the close to home bedrock whereupon the characters could fabricate their prospects. The goal of relational intricacies was not a clean decision but rather an acknowledgment of the persevering through integrates that bound ages. The tradition of familial bonds, conveying both the heaviness of history and the commitment of progression, turned into a foundation whereupon the characters could incline as they wandered into the unexplored world.

In the more extensive setting of the district that filled in as the background for these entwined predeterminations, the account conclusion stretched out to the difficulties looked by the local area. Monetary difficulties, social divisions, and ecological worries had been imposing enemies, and the characters played dynamic parts in resolving these issues. The conclusion was not an idealistic goal of all issues but rather an impression of the strength and aggregate endeavors that had started to prove to be fruitful.

Monetary rejuvenation, prodded by enterprising undertakings and local area drives, infused imperativeness into the district. Private ventures flourished, making a far reaching influence that supported neighborhood economies and gave potential open doors to feasible development. The conclusion of monetary battles stamped not the finish of difficulties but rather a change in direction — an affirmation that the district could cut out a future characterized by thriving and shared achievement.

Social union, once stressed by contrasts and errors, saw a steady repairing of the common texture. The characters, exemplifying the soul of solidarity and understanding, became influencers inside their networks. Festivities of variety, consideration, and shared values turned into the standard, cultivating a feeling of having a place that rose above individual foundations. The conclusion of social divisions proclaimed the beginning of a more interconnected and amicable local area.

Ecological protection, a string woven all through the story, saw the products of aggregate endeavors in the district. The once-corrupted scenes went through rebuilding, and maintainable practices became imbued locally's ethos. The conclusion of ecological worries was not a last victory but rather an acknowledgment of the continuous obligation to stewardship and the comprehension that the strength of the district was complicatedly connected to the prosperity of its occupants.

As the characters remained on the cliff of conclusion, their look moved in the direction of the skyline where fresh starts anticipated. The commitment of the obscure, touched with both expectation and vulnerability, enticed them forward. The conclusion of one section was not the finish of their accounts but rather an introduction to the experiences that lay ahead.

The hero, having risen up out of the cauldron of self-improvement, conveyed the insight of involvement into the unknown domains representing things to come. The illustrations took in, the scars procured, and the versatility found turned into a compass directing the way forward. The conclusion of past vulnerabilities denoted the kickoff of another section — one characterized by the hero's advancing feeling of direction and a steadfast obligation to add to the advancement of the local area.

The supporting characters, as well, remained at the limit of fresh starts. Kinships produced in the flames of shared difficulties became establishments whereupon future joint efforts could be constructed. The conclusion of relational contentions was not the finish of their accounts but rather an introduction to coalitions that would shape the aggregate fate of the locale. As the characters looked toward the future, a feeling of kinship and common perspective implanted the air.

In the domain of affection and association, the conclusion of heartfelt entrapments was not the last section but rather a progress to a story of shared goals and common development. The characters, having explored the intricacies of connections, conveyed with them the insight acquired from the preliminaries of affection. The commitment of fresh starts held the potential for more profound associations, shared dreams, and a continuation of the multifaceted dance of the human heart.

Relational peculiarities, having gone through the cauldron of goal and recuperating, remained as strong points of support whereupon the characters could incline. The conclusion of familial struggles was not the finish of generational stories but rather a reaffirmation of the persevering through attaches that bound the characters to their foundations. The commitment of fresh starts inside the setting of family conveyed with it the expectation for proceeded with development, understanding, and the passing down of customs that characterized the locale's personality.

The more extensive district, having endured financial difficulties, social divisions, and ecological worries, entered another period of its account. The conclusion of past battles denoted a defining moment — an acknowledgment that the local area had the organization to shape its fate. The commitment of fresh starts for the area lay in the aggregate obligation to supportability, inclusivity, and shared success.

As the sun plunged lower not too far off, creating long shaded areas that extended toward the future, a significant feeling of conclusion encompassed the characters and the locale they called home.

The past, with every one of its hardships, had been recognized, comprehended, and incorporated into the story of aggregate development. The commitment of fresh starts was not a far off illusion but rather a substantial reality, enticing the characters to step strikingly into the following parts of their lives.

In the end snapshots of this complex story, as the characters ready to set out on the excursions that looked for them, there waited a reverberation of trust — a conviction that the locale, similar to its occupants, held inside it the potential for proceeded with change and recharging. The conclusion was not a certainty but rather a snapshot of reflection, a breath before the following inward breath of potential outcomes.

The commitment of fresh starts, reverberating in the hearts of the characters and the locale, conveyed with it the hopefulness brought into the world from the illustrations of the past. The stories, interconnected and interlaced, framed an embroidery that stretched out past the current second, venturing into the future where the strings of development, flexibility, and shared goals would keep on forming the predetermination of the characters and the district they called home.

As the scene embraced the shades of nightfall, a feeling of conclusion settled over the characters and the locale. However, inside that conclusion, there existed the everlasting commitment of day break — a commitment that each finishing was nevertheless a preface to a fresh start, and that the excursion, with every one of its intricacies and miracles, would keep on unfurling in manners yet concealed. The characters, with hearts overflowing with encounters and eyes fixed not too far off, ventured forward into the hug of fresh starts, prepared to prearrange the following sections of their interlaced fates.

The sun plunged underneath the skyline, projecting its warm shine over the extensive scene, as the characters in this unpredictable account remained at the edge of fresh starts. The embroidery of their lives, woven with strings of intricacy, development, and shared predeterminations, had arrived at a snapshot of conclusion, giving way to the commitment of new beginnings and strange excursions. The characters, having crossed different circular segments of improvement, wound up on the cusp of an aggregate and individual development that would rethink their lives and the locale they called home.

In the domain of self-awareness and self-revelation, the characters rose up out of the cauldron of their encounters changed and illuminated. The hero, once questionable and reluctant, presently remained with a freshly discovered certainty, a demonstration of the strength of the human soul despite difficulty. The excursion of self-revelation, set apart by contemplation and snapshots of weakness, had prompted a significant comprehension of personality and reason. As the hero looked into the figurative mirror, the reflection was one of genuineness, strength, and an extended identity mindfulness.

Going with the hero were a large group of supporting characters, each having gone through their own transformation. Companions developed into mainstays of help, tutors gave direction, and foes, once saw as snags, uncovered themselves as impetuses for change. The conclusion of their singular curves was not just the tying of remaining details but rather a festival of the perplexing dance of connections and the significant effect they had on molding the characters' predeterminations.

Topics of adoration and association, woven complicatedly into the story, arrived at a finish in the last ventures. Heartfelt snares, when a wellspring of contention and disarray, tracked down goal in the embroidery of understanding and common development. The connections that endured the everyday hardships and adversity arose more grounded, their bonds developed by shared encounters and a common obligation to exploring the intricacies of adoration.

Family, a foundation of the characters' lives, assumed a vital part in the story conclusion. Compromises, pardoning, and the mending of wounds framed the close to home bedrock whereupon the characters could assemble their prospects. The goal of relational intricacies was not a perfect determination but rather an acknowledgment of the persevering through integrates that bound ages. The tradition of familial bonds, conveying both the heaviness of history and the commitment of progression, turned into a foundation whereupon the characters could incline as they wandered into the unexplored world.

In the more extensive setting of the district that filled in as the background for these entwined fates, the story conclusion reached out to the difficulties looked by the local area. Financial difficulties, social divisions, and ecological worries had been considerable foes, and the characters played dynamic parts in resolving these issues. The conclusion was not an idealistic goal of all issues but rather an impression of the strength and aggregate endeavors that had started to prove to be fruitful.

Financial renewal, started by pioneering tries and local area drives, infused essentialness into the district. Private ventures flourished, making a far reaching influence that reinforced nearby economies and given open doors to economical development. The conclusion of financial battles stamped not the finish of difficulties but rather a change in direction — an affirmation that the district could cut out a future characterized by thriving and shared achievement.

Social union, once stressed by contrasts and false impressions, saw a progressive patching of the collective texture. The characters, epitomizing the soul of solidarity and understanding, became influencers inside their networks. Festivities of variety, incorporation, and shared values turned into the standard, cultivating a feeling of having a place that rose above individual foundations. The conclusion of social divisions proclaimed the beginning of a more interconnected and amicable local area.

Natural preservation, a string woven all through the story, saw the products of aggregate endeavors in the locale. The once-debased scenes went through reclamation, and feasible practices became imbued locally's ethos. The conclusion of ecological worries was not a last victory but rather an acknowledgment of the continuous obligation to stewardship and the comprehension that the soundness of the locale was complicatedly connected to the prosperity of its occupants.

As the characters remained on the slope of conclusion, their look moved in the direction of the skyline where fresh starts anticipated. The commitment of the obscure, touched with both expectation and vulnerability, enticed them forward. The conclusion of one section was not the finish of their accounts but rather an introduction to the experiences that lay ahead.

The hero, having risen up out of the cauldron of self-awareness, conveyed the insight of involvement into the unfamiliar domains representing things to come. The examples took in, the scars procured, and the flexibility found turned into a compass directing the way forward. The conclusion of past vulnerabilities denoted the launch of another section

— one characterized by the hero's developing feeling of direction and an enduring obligation to add to the advancement of the local area.

The supporting characters, as well, remained at the limit of fresh starts. Kinships produced in the flames of shared difficulties became establishments whereupon future joint efforts could be fabricated. The conclusion of relational struggles was not the finish of their accounts but rather a preface to unions that would shape the aggregate predetermination of the locale. As the characters looked toward the future, a feeling of fellowship and common perspective implanted the air.

In the domain of affection and association, the conclusion of heartfelt ensnarements was not the last section but rather a progress to a story of shared goals and common development. The characters, having explored the intricacies of connections, conveyed with them the insight acquired from the preliminaries of adoration. The commitment of fresh starts held the potential for more profound associations, shared dreams, and a continuation of the many-sided dance of the human heart.

Relational intricacies, having gone through the pot of goal and recuperating, remained as tough points of support whereupon the characters could incline. The conclusion of familial contentions was not the finish of generational stories but rather a reaffirmation of the getting through attaches that bound the characters to their foundations. The commitment of fresh starts inside the setting of family conveyed with it the expectation for proceeded with development, understanding, and the passing down of customs that characterized the area's personality.

The more extensive district, having endured financial difficulties, social divisions, and ecological worries, entered another period of its account. The conclusion of past battles denoted a defining moment — an acknowledgment that the local area had the organization to shape its predetermination. The commitment of fresh starts for the district lay in the aggregate obligation to manageability, inclusivity, and shared flourishing.

As the characters remained on the incline of conclusion, their look moved in the direction of the skyline where fresh starts anticipated.

The commitment of the obscure, touched with both expectation and vulnerability, coaxed them forward. The conclusion of one part was not the finish of their accounts but rather a preface to the undertakings that lay ahead.

The hero, having risen up out of the pot of self-improvement, conveyed the insight of involvement into the unknown regions representing things to come. The illustrations took in, the scars procured, and the versatility found turned into a compass directing the way forward. The conclusion of past vulnerabilities denoted the kickoff of another section — one characterized by the hero's developing feeling of direction and an immovable obligation to add to the advancement of the local area.

The supporting characters, as well, remained at the edge of fresh starts. Fellowships produced in the flames of shared difficulties became establishments whereupon future coordinated efforts could be assembled. The conclusion of relational struggles was not the finish of their accounts but rather an introduction to coalitions that would shape the aggregate predetermination of the district. As the characters looked toward the future, a feeling of brotherhood and common perspective injected the air.

In the domain of adoration and association, the conclusion of heartfelt ensnarements was not the last part but rather a progress to a story of shared yearnings and common development. The characters, having explored the intricacies of connections, conveyed with them the insight acquired from the preliminaries of affection. The commitment of fresh starts held the potential for more profound associations, shared dreams, and a continuation of the complicated dance of the human heart.

Relational peculiarities, having gone through the pot of goal and recuperating, remained as tough points of support whereupon the characters could incline. The conclusion of familial struggles was not the finish of generational stories but rather a reaffirmation of the getting through attaches that bound the characters to their foundations. The commitment of fresh starts inside the setting of family conveyed with it the expectation for proceeded with development, understanding, and the passing down of customs that characterized the district's personality.

The more extensive district, having endured financial difficulties, social divisions, and ecological worries, entered another period of its story. The conclusion of past battles denoted a defining moment — an acknowledgment that the local area had the organization to shape its fate.

The commitment of fresh starts for the district lay in the aggregate obligation to maintainability, inclusivity, and shared success.

As the characters remained on the slope of conclusion, their look moved in the direction of the skyline where fresh starts anticipated. The commitment of the obscure, touched with both expectation and vulnerability, allured them forward. The conclusion of one section was not the finish of their accounts but rather an introduction to the undertakings that lay ahead.

The hero, having risen up out of the cauldron of self-improvement, conveyed the insight of involvement into the strange domains representing things to come. The examples took in, the scars procured, and the versatility found turned into a compass directing the way forward. The conclusion of past vulnerabilities denoted the kickoff of another part — one characterized by the hero's advancing feeling of direction and a relentless obligation to add to the improvement of the local area.

The supporting characters, as well, remained at the limit of fresh starts. Kinships manufactured in the flames of shared difficulties became establishments whereupon future coordinated efforts could be fabricated. The conclusion of relational contentions was not the finish of their accounts but rather an introduction to collusions that would shape the aggregate fate of the district. As the characters looked toward the future, a feeling of kinship and common perspective injected the air.

In the domain of affection and association, the conclusion of heartfelt snares was not the last part but rather a progress to a story of shared goals and common development. The characters, having explored the intricacies of connections, conveyed with them the insight acquired from the preliminaries of adoration. The commitment of fresh starts held the potential for more profound associations, shared dreams, and a continuation of the multifaceted dance of the human heart.

Relational peculiarities, having gone through the cauldron of goal and recuperating, remained as versatile support points whereupon the characters could incline. The conclusion of familial struggles was not the finish of generational stories but rather a reaffirmation of the getting through attaches that bound the characters to their underlying foundations. The commitment of fresh starts inside the setting of family conveyed with it the expectation for proceeded with development, understanding, and the passing down of customs that characterized the area's personality.

The more extensive locale, having endured financial difficulties, social divisions, and natural worries, entered another period of its account. The conclusion of past battles denoted a defining moment — an acknowledgment that the local area had the organization to shape its fate. The commitment of fresh starts for the area lay in the aggregate obligation to maintainability, inclusivity, and shared flourishing.

As the characters remained on the slope of conclusion, their look moved in the direction of the skyline where fresh starts anticipated. The commitment of the obscure, touched with both expectation and vulnerability, enticed them forward. The conclusion of one section was not the finish of their accounts but rather a preface to the experiences that lay ahead.

The hero, having risen up out of the pot of self-improvement, conveyed the insight of involvement into the unfamiliar regions representing things to come. The examples took in, the scars procured, and the versatility found turned into a compass directing the way forward. The conclusion of past vulnerabilities denoted the launch of another section — one characterized by the hero's advancing feeling of direction and a steadfast obligation to add to the improvement of the local area.

The supporting characters, as well, remained at the edge of fresh starts. Fellowships fashioned in the flames of shared difficulties became establishments whereupon future joint efforts could be fabricated. The conclusion of relational contentions was not the finish of their accounts but rather a preface to coalitions that would shape the aggregate predetermination of the locale. As the characters looked toward the future, a feeling of fellowship and common perspective imbued the air.

In the domain of adoration and association, the conclusion of heartfelt traps was not the last section but rather a progress to a story of shared yearnings and common development. The characters, having explored the intricacies of connections, conveyed with them the insight acquired from the preliminaries of affection. The commitment of fresh starts held the potential for more profound associations, shared dreams, and a continuation of the perplexing dance of the human heart.

Relational intricacies, having gone through the pot of goal and mending, remained as strong points of support whereupon the characters could incline. The conclusion of familial contentions was not the finish of generational stories but rather a reaffirmation of the getting through attaches that bound the characters to their underlying foundations. The commitment of fresh starts inside the setting of family conveyed with it the expectation for proceeded with development, understanding, and the passing down of customs that characterized the district's personality.

The more extensive locale, having endured monetary difficulties, social divisions, and ecological worries, entered another period of its story. The conclusion of past battles denoted a defining moment — an acknowledgment that the local area had the organization to shape its predetermination. The commitment of fresh starts for the district lay in the aggregate obligation to manageability, inclusivity, and shared thriving.

As the characters remained on the slope of conclusion, their look moved in the direction of the skyline where fresh starts anticipated. The commitment of the obscure, touched with both expectation and vulnerability, allured them forward. The conclusion of one section was not the finish of their accounts but rather a preamble to the undertakings that lay ahead.

The hero, having risen up out of the cauldron of self-awareness, conveyed the insight of involvement into the unknown domains representing things to come. The examples took in, the scars procured, and the strength found turned into a compass directing the way forward. The conclusion of past vulnerabilities denoted the kickoff of another section — one characterized by the hero's advancing feeling of direction and a steadfast obligation to add to the advancement of the local area.

The supporting characters, as well, remained at the edge of fresh starts. Companionships fashioned in the flames of shared difficulties became establishments whereupon future coordinated efforts could be assembled. The conclusion of relational contentions was not the finish of their accounts but rather a preface to unions that would shape the aggregate predetermination of the locale. As the characters looked toward the future, a feeling of brotherhood and common perspective mixed the air.

In the domain of adoration and association, the conclusion of heartfelt ensnarements was not the last part but rather a change to a story of shared desires and common development. The characters, having explored the intricacies of connections, conveyed with them the insight acquired from the preliminaries of adoration. The commitment of fresh starts held the potential for more profound associations, shared dreams, and a continuation of the mind boggling dance of the human heart.

Relational intricacies, having gone through the pot of goal and mending, remained as tough support points whereupon the characters could incline. The conclusion of familial contentions was not the finish of generational stories but rather a reaffirmation of the getting through attaches that bound the characters to their underlying foundations. The commitment of fresh starts inside the setting of family conveyed with it the expectation for proceeded with development, understanding, and the passing down of customs that characterized the locale's personality.

The more extensive district, having endured monetary difficulties, social divisions, and natural worries, entered another period of its account. The conclusion of past battles denoted a defining moment — an acknowledgment that the local area had the organization to shape its predetermination. The commitment of fresh starts for the area lay in the aggregate obligation to maintainability, inclusivity, and shared flourishing.

As the characters remained on the cliff of conclusion, their look moved in the direction of the skyline where fresh starts anticipated. The commitment of the obscure, touched with both expectation and vulnerability, enticed them forward. The conclusion of one section was not the finish of their accounts but rather an introduction to the experiences that lay ahead.

The hero, having risen up out of the pot of self-improvement, conveyed the insight of involvement into the unfamiliar regions representing things to come. The examples took in, the scars procured, and the flexibility found turned into a compass directing the way forward. The conclusion of past vulnerabilities denoted the launch of another section — one characterized by the hero's developing feeling of direction and a faithful obligation to add to the advancement of the local area.

www.ingramcontent.com/pod-product-compliance
Lightning Source LLC
LaVergne TN
LVHW021047100526
838202LV00079B/4659